Theater Careers

Also by Jan W. Greenberg

THEATER BUSINESS

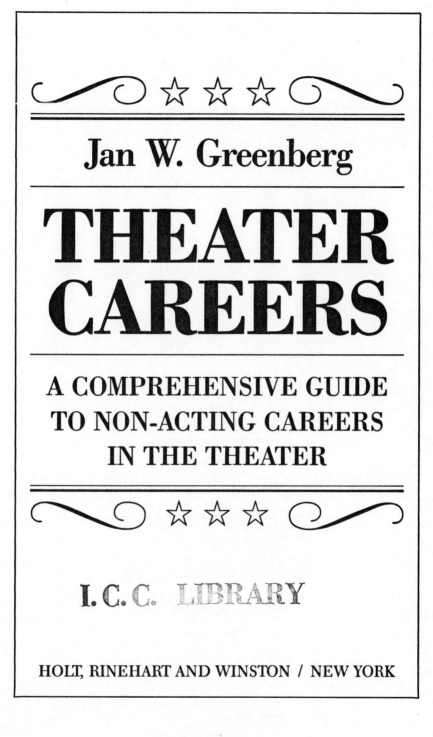

Jan W. Greenberg

THEATER CAREERS

A COMPREHENSIVE GUIDE TO NON-ACTING CAREERS IN THE THEATER

HOLT, RINEHART AND WINSTON / NEW YORK

To Lester

Copyright © 1983 by Jan W. Greenberg
All rights reserved, including the right to reproduce
this book or portions thereof in any form.
Published by Holt, Rinehart and Winston,
383 Madison Avenue, New York, New York 10017.
Published simultaneously in Canada by Holt, Rinehart
and Winston of Canada, Limited.

Library of Congress Cataloging in Publication Data

Greenberg, Jan W. (Jan Weingarten)
Theater careers.
Includes index.
Summary: Discusses backstage careers in the theater
such as those of producer, manager, director, press
agent, casting director, musician, lighting designer,
propertyman, carpenter, and dresser. Includes
interviews with persons working in various fields.
1. Theater—Vocational guidance—Juvenile literature.
[1. Theater—Vocational guidance. 2. Vocational guidance.]
I. Title
PN2074.G73 1983   792'.023'73   83-4386
ISBN 0-03-061568-2

First Edition

Printed in the United States of America
1 3 5 7 9 10 8 6 4 2

ISBN 0-03-061568-2

Contents

Theater Careers

Introduction

When people consider work in the theater, most immediately think of acting. However, a glance at the end credits of a theatrical program will show a list of support personnel including such diverse positions as stage manager, press agent, manager, wardrobe supervisor, and advertising account executive. So for someone who wants a life in the theater backstage instead of onstage, work exists. However, there are some truths of theatrical life about which you should be forewarned before embarking upon a career in the theater.

• You will probably not get rich (or even wealthy). Playwright Robert Anderson once said: "You can make a killing in the theater but you can't make a living in the theater." He was referring to the commercial theater, but the inverse is true for not-for-profit theater. You can make a living (although often a rather small one), but you certainly won't make a killing.

• You are likely to have periods of unemployment.

• If you work in the commercial theater, you will almost certainly have to join a union or professional society and fulfill specific requirements for membership. It's rarely easy to do so.

• You will probably have to travel in order to find work or simply to advance in your career.

• Your hours will not be 9:00 A.M. to 5:00 P.M. Nor will you work Monday through Friday with holidays off. Theater hours are usually other people's nonworking hours.

• Working conditions will not be plush. Your career may be glamorous, but the place where you work won't be.

Despite these negatives, working in the theater has a magic and excitement uniquely its own. Truly a collaborative enterprise, everyone—from the flyman who raises the curtain to the person who painstakingly prepares the music for the orchestra—shares in the results that appear onstage.

The "nine to five" mentality doesn't exist in the theater. Rather, the theater retains a special mystique and, almost without exception, those who spend their lives within it remain stagestruck, unable to envision any other life.

This book identifies non-acting professions in the theater. Entrance criteria, union requirements, and necessary professional skills are described. But the book's primary intent is to impart a sense of what "life in the theater" is really about, through interviews and profiles of working professionals in both the commercial and not-for-profit theater. Representatives of the creative and business sectors talk about their work—how they got started, what they do, and what the theatrical life means to them.

A Life in the Theater

People usually focus on New York City and, most particularly, the thirty-nine commercial theaters or houses, as they are called, in which Broadway shows play. When thinking about the theater, it is here that most aspiring theater professionals hope to work. However, there is theater throughout the United States. Indeed, you are more likely to have year-round employment at one of the nation's not-for-profit, regional theaters that operate on a twelve-month basis than in commercial Broadway or off-Broadway ventures. On Broadway work lasts only as long as the show does. And it is not uncommon for a show to open and close within a few weeks, sometimes even the same night. The *Annies* and *A Chorus Lines* of this business are the exceptions.

Commercial Theater

The commercial theater is a profit-making enterprise. Today, the commercial theater is almost exclusively limited to Broadway and off-Broadway, although large cities such as Boston, Philadelphia, and Los Angeles also house commercial productions, usually those that are trying out prior to a New York Broadway opening or shows that have completed a successful run on Broadway and are on tour.

3

Since commercial theater productions support themselves through earned income (ticket sales), commercial productions are most often presented for mass appeal. Producers and investors hope to realize a profit from the production. With few exceptions, commercial theater is presented in union houses and only union personnel are permitted to work on the productions.

Unions

Unions are a potent force in the commercial theater. Almost every job comes under the jurisdiction of a union or professional society. These organizations mandate minimum fees or salaries, working conditions, the number of personnel a producer must hire, and the specific duties their members may or may not perform. A producer and theater owner mounting a commercial production will sign contracts with personnel representing at least twelve trade and professional organizations by the time the show opens.

These unions were founded to protect employees in a business where not only is money lost most of the time, but the show, the business, can cease to exist overnight. Prior to the unionization of the commercial theater, situations existed in which fees weren't paid and actors and other show personnel were stranded in the middle of the country after their shows closed unexpectedly. Aspiring workers were often so eager for theatrical jobs that employment was too often determined by a willingness to work long hours under grueling conditions, rather than by skills or qualifications.

Unions exist to protect workers in a business that is precarious even in the best of times. However, there are many more people who want to work in the theater than there are jobs. Many of the unions make it difficult for new members to gain admittance and thus employment. It is often a Catch-22 situation: you cannot work if you are not in the union, but you cannot get into the union unless you have work.

Unions are a fact of life, which must be addressed when contemplating a professional life in the theater. Entry requirements vary from union to union. Some simply require payment of a membership fee, while others require a lengthy apprenticeship and the successful completion of an examination. Even within a union's locals (chapters with jurisdiction over specific geographic areas), entrance criteria differ. This book discusses union policies where applicable, but readers wishing to join unions regulating theatrical work will have to contact them directly in order to receive up-to-date guidance on union policies. (The appendix lists all theatrical union contracts.)

Broadway and Off-Broadway

There are thirty-nine Broadway houses, four "middle" Broadway houses, and thirty-eight off-Broadway houses. Many of these off-Broadway theaters are occupied full-time by New York City's not-for-profit producing organizations, which work under special union contracts. The commercial theaters are categorized by seating capacity and location. People are hired to work on individual productions, although each theater maintains a staff that works at the theater when it is housing a show.

In the Broadway and off-Broadway commercial theater, the producer hires all production personnel and the theater owner all theater personnel. If the show is a hit, everyone stands to benefit. Those who work on maintaining the show— the stage manager, press agent, wardrobe supervisor, stage hands, etc.—are assured ongoing employment and weekly paychecks. Those who have participated in creating the show—the playwright, designers, director—receive a percentage of the production's weekly gross receipts. This payment is called a royalty and is in addition to the fee paid before opening. If the show fails and closes, everyone connected with it is out of work and, after a set amount of time, the production company is dissolved.

Touring Theater

There are three kinds of national touring companies in the commercial theater: the first-class productions of Broadway hit shows, "bus and truck," and arena or star packages.

When a producer secures the rights to produce a play, in addition to the Broadway or off-Broadway production, he* can also produce first-class national companies and a London production. A hit show, especially if it is a musical that has broad-based appeal, generates companies that tour the nation, playing in the commercial theaters of large cities. Increasingly, major hits such as *A Chorus Line*, *Evita*, and *Sophisticated Ladies* have standing companies that open in major cities such as Washington, D.C., Los Angeles, and Boston for open-ended engagements. These "superhits" often have several companies performing throughout the United States and in London, in addition to the Broadway production. They provide work for both those who travel with the show and those who reside in cities in which the production plays.

"Bus and truck" are companies that crisscross the nation, playing what are known as split weeks (four days in one town and three in another) or even one-night stands. Bus-and-

---

* Throughout the book the pronoun "he" is used solely for convenience. The positions described in this book can be, and for the most part are, held by both men and women.

truck companies tour smaller towns and cities and often play college campuses. They are called bus and truck because the sets and heavy equipment are transported by truck and the cast and company travel by bus.

Reminiscent of the theater companies that traversed the nation years ago, bus-and-truck tours are not easy. Usually the production travels at night after the performance and sets up in the theater for the next performance early the next morning. Bus-and-truck rights are sold by the producer to independent producing organizations that mount, manage, and book the shows throughout the nation.

Arena shows and star packages are traveling attractions that are built around a theme (Walt Disney on Parade, Ice Capades) or highlight a well-known personality (Steve Lawrence and Eydie Gormé, Ruby Keeler in *No, No, Nanette*). Arena shows play in large auditoriums and amphitheaters. Star packages usually tour on what is often called the summer circuit. These are the seasonal tents, barns, and playhouses located near resort areas and open during the summer months. Dinner theaters and enclosed amphitheaters located primarily near suburban areas book these shows throughout the year.

Dinner Theater
Located primarily in suburban areas, dinner theaters usually present musicals, light comedies, or star packages. The price of admission includes a meal, parking, and the show. There are chains of dinner theaters that retain permanent staffs of stage managers, bookers, and production workers, often rotating shows from theater to theater. Some dinner theaters come under union jurisdiction, but nonunion personnel can be hired in certain positions.

Industrial Shows

While not technically theater, industrial shows are live performances underwritten and produced by businesses to highlight and describe their products. They are frequently performed at conventions or at company sales conferences and are designed to excite people and build enthusiasm for a company's products. Industrial shows use many of the same personnel as theatrical presentations and offer short-term, usually highly paid, employment.

Not-for-Profit Theater

This is theater that doesn't expect to make a profit from its productions. It is supported by government grants, foundations, corporations, and individual donors who are allowed to deduct the amount of their contribution as a tax write-off.

Regional Theater

This is also called professional resident theater or repertory theater, although, for most of these companies, the name "repertory" is really a misnomer. In a true repertory company, the same group of actors work together on a number of plays that are performed with actors rotating parts. There are approximately 160 regional not-for-profit theaters located in the United States and New York City. The majority were founded during the 1960s.

Most of the regional theaters are members of the League of Resident Theaters (LORT) and employ both union and non-union members. Actors and stage managers are usually members of Actors' Equity Association, the actors' union, and most designers work under guidelines set by the United

Scenic Artists. But for other personnel, union membership is not a requirement.

The regional theaters offer professional theater to areas of the country that might not otherwise have access to live theater. Because they are not-for-profit and continuously producing organizations, they can present the kinds of plays, such as classics and forgotten works from the past, that profit-making ventures cannot. In addition, new playwrights have the opportunity to see their work presented. Most of these theaters have internship and educational programs and many tour, bringing live theater to those who might be otherwise unable to see it.

Increasingly, regional theaters play an important role in commercial production. Most dramatic plays that appear in the commercial theater these days had their genesis in regional theater. These works include such recent Pulitzer Prize–winning plays as *The Shadow Box, The Gin Game, Talley's Folly,* and *Crimes of the Heart.* Even some musicals such as *Annie* had their roots in these theaters. The not-for-profit arena has the time to nurture a developing production and can take a chance on an unknown playwright in a way that a high-stake commercial venture simply cannot.

Although plays go from the not-for-profit realm to the commercial theater, there is not much back-and-forth movement of personnel. Directors, designers, and playwrights do work both commercially and in the not-for-profit theater. But because of union requirements and different professional skills, management and administrative personnel usually remain in one or the other.

Summer Stock
These are producing organizations that operate in resort areas during the summer months. A few are strictly commercial

enterprises, booking star packages amd touring musicals, but most others produce shows using a company of resident actors and technical and artistic personnel.

Off-Off Broadway

This is not-for-profit theater that is located almost exclusively in New York City. It is a term encompassing a range of activity from the small, ongoing professional producing organizations that are not under union jurisdiction, to the showcase productions that are presented to highlight the work of actors, directors, and playwrights.

University Theater

University theaters are producing organizations that are affiliated with universities or drama schools. Utilizing both professional and student actors, directors, and designers, they not only present fully mounted theatrical productions but provide practical experience for student technical and administrative personnel.

Community Theater

These are local theater companies in small towns and communities throughout the nation. They range from purely amateur groups to established companies in which professionals are hired to work with local amateurs in presenting shows.

Children's Theater

These are standing theater groups that produce shows for children. Many are supported by government and foundation grants and regularly tour their localities, performing in schools, churches, and institutions.

The Commercial Producer and the Not-for-Profit Artistic Director

All forms of theater have someone who functions as producer. The producer is responsible for the entire process of production, starting with selection of the property to be presented. If the project must be developed (for instance, a script adapted from a book or an original musical requiring the collaboration of composer, lyricist, and librettist), the producer oversees the work both financially and artistically. He decides when the show will open and when it will close. He hires and fires all artistic and management personnel. The producer chooses the theater where the production will be performed and must raise all funds necessary to finance the show.

The type of theater determines the specific tasks of the producer. Dinner theater and summer stock operations that book star packages require different producing skills from commercial and regional theater, in which new productions are often developed and presented. The former requires more business skills and access to a good booking organization, whereas the latter calls for specific theatrical skills and background. There are further distinctions between producing in the commercial theater and producing in the not-for-profit realm. In the commercial theater the producer presents each show as a single entity. In the not-for-profit theater the producer is called the artistic director. He both directs productions and selects an entire season of work to be presented.

The Commercial Theater Producer

Producing in the commercial theater is theoretically one of the few businesses in which you can start at the top. All you need is money and a property to produce. However, good producing requires knowledge, and most successful producers have spent years working at various theatrical jobs learning the business. They know which theaters are best for certain shows; what the best timing is for the actual production of a property; which people work best together; if it is better to go out of town before opening on Broadway; how the theatrical unions and professional societies work; and even the basic ways in which increasingly technologically advanced stage equipment operate.

In the commercial theater, shows are traditionally financed by investors. Often called angels or backers, these investors are, in fact, limited partners in a special arrangement called a limited partnership company. This company is set up solely to produce the show and holds individual investors responsible only for the amount of their agreed-upon investment. If the show makes a profit, the investors pay taxes on the income received as they would on any other income. If the show loses money, the investors can deduct this loss for income tax purposes.

The producer, the name publicly associated with the show,

is the general partner. The limited partners divide fifty percent of any profits realized by the production proportionally according to the amount of their investment. The producer/general partner receives the other fifty percent of any profits. He also takes a weekly fee, which is either a percentage of the gross box office receipts, a set amount of money, or both, toward office expenses while the show is in production.

Most producers do not finance shows out of their own pocket and rely on outside backing. The limited partnership prospectus that describes the show and its creators and contains both the capitalization and operating budgets includes a section entitled "The Risk to Investors," stating that the vast majority of commercial theatrical enterprises fail. While theater investors know that the majority of shows never recoup the production costs, let alone make a profit, they have the right to assume their money is not stupidly or badly spent. Good producing can make the difference between a real debacle where a show runs out of money during rehearsal and cannot open and a well-produced failure.

Years ago, the business of producing in the theater was different. Many more plays were produced each year. For instance, during the 1927–28 season, a still-standing record of 264 plays opened, costing an average of $10,000 to produce. Sixty theaters housed these plays and ticket prices ranged from 65¢ to $1.10 a seat. A show that played 100 performances was considered a hit.

In those days, many producers maintained offices. They had staffs to read scripts, casting directors to fill the roles for each show, publicists to promote the shows, and managers to oversee business and technical details. These producers also had rosters of investors who were willing to bankroll their shows. In many ways, although salaries and working conditions were not as good as they are today, it was easier to break into the theater and, once in, maintain more or less steady employment. Producing was a real business and, for some, profitable enough to work at on a full-time basis.

Today, Broadway shows cost over $750,000 to produce if they are dramas, and well over $1.5 million if they are musicals. Approximately fifty-five shows open each year, with ticket prices ranging from $50 to $15 (for the rear balcony at a Wednesday matinee). It can take years to pay off a show's production expenses and this often occurs only after a movie or recording sale has been made, or the show is such a blockbuster that national and touring companies take to the road.

Since producing in the commercial theater has become so expensive, most shows are financed through a combination of individual investors and funds from corporate entertainment complexes, such as film and recording companies. These companies join as coproducers, becoming general partners and also realizing certain benefits if the show is a hit, such as the first rights to a possible film or recording. They become producers so that they can share in all of the possible subsidiary deals generated by a hit show. Subsidiary rights are all the uses of a production other than the actual presentation and include movies, television specials, tie-ins such as books, T-shirts, and other promotional merchandise.

Today, only a few producers maintain full-time operating offices. And of those who do, most are involved in theatrical enterprises other than producing. Elizabeth McCann and Nelle Nugent produced *The Elephant Man, Dracula, Mornings at Seven, Amadeus,* and *Nicholas Nickelby.* They are also general managers, managing the shows they produce and those of other producers.

The Shubert Organization were among the producers of *Ain't Misbehavin', Dancin', Dreamgirls,* and *The Gin Game.* They own and operate sixteen of Broadway's most desirable theaters and own a half interest in one other as well. They also own theaters outside New York and are the most powerful organization in the commercial theater today.

The Nederlander Organization owns ten Broadway theaters and others throughout the country. They were among the producers of *Annie, Lena Horne: The Lady and Her Music,* and *Woman of the Year,* and they are increasingly active in the New York commercial theater as producers. But along with the Shuberts, they are in the real estate business.

Commercial Broadway production is so expensive that if one looks at the list of producers for a single show, there will usually be a combination of individuals and corporations. Even "competitors" like the Nederlander Organization, the Shuberts, and McCann/Nugent can be found jointly producing shows on Broadway.

Each listed producer has either invested his own company's or individual funds into the show or has raised a certain percentage of the necessary monies for production. Usually, however, only one or two individuals devote their full time to the actual business of producing and the day-to-day decisions. Some examples of these joint producing ventures include:

Amadeus—The Shubert Organization, Elizabeth McCann and Nelle Nugent, and Roger Berlind (a former investment banker).

Dreamgirls—Michael Bennett (its director-choreographer and creator of *A Chorus Line*), Bob Avian (Bennett's associate choreographer and director), David Geffen (head of his own recording company, Geffen Records, which recorded the *Dreamgirls* cast album), and the Shubert Organization.

Lately, most straight plays have come to Broadway via one of the nation's regional theaters or London. With the exception of musicals, many of which are collaborative enterprises

and are developed under the auspices of commercial producers, straight plays are picked up by what can be called
merchandising producers and brought to Broadway. The
originating theater participates in any profits realized, although this share is usually no more than two percent. The
commercial producer must still raise the funds necessary to
present the show on Broadway.

Morton Gottlieb is a Broadway producer. His productions include *Tribute, Same Time, Next Year, Romantic Comedy,*
and *The Killing of Sister George.*

* * *

"I always wanted to be a producer. I was lucky in that my
mother's aunt Minnie married a man named Jake Openhei-
mer. He owned the Lyric Theater [now a run-down movie
house] on Forty-Second Street, which is among those slated
for renovation. Starting at the age of six, I went to the theater
every Saturday and Wednesday matinee. I saw everything at
the Lyric, and my uncle got tickets for other shows, usually
musicals, but sometimes a serious play.

"At the Lyric, I sat in the box office before the curtain went
up and the manager's office during intermission. After the
show, I'd go backstage. I thought it would be fun to be like
Florenz Ziegfeld, whose shows were produced at the Lyric
and whom I met backstage. So when I was six years old, that's
what I decided to do, and everything I did after that was
towards going into the Broadway theater and becoming a
producer."

Gottlieb attended Yale University, taking courses in the
Drama School. He worked for a New Jersey newspaper and
became a press agent in New York City, working at an agency
that handled nightclubs and entertainers.

"That wasn't what I really wanted to be doing, but I used it as a way to meet people and do things that would relate to Broadway. Along the way, one of the offices with which I was associated did the publicity for Gertrude Lawrence [one of the theater's legendary actresses who originated the role of Anna in *The King and I*]. I became very close to her and through her husband, Dick Aldredge, became a manager with Theatre Incorporated. I shifted at that time from publicity to being a manager, working first as a company manager and later as a general manager."

As a general manager, Gottlieb managed shows for some of Broadway's busiest producers in the 1950s. He served as general manager for the American Shakespeare Festival in Stratford, Connecticut. In the 1960s, Gottlieb started to work with producer Helen Bonfils, a former actress who became publisher of the *Denver Post*.

"One day, she said, 'Oh, go out and find a play and I'll put up the money.' I found *Enter Laughing* and it turned out to be a big success. It ran for over a year on Broadway, toured, and had a movie sale. After she died, I started to take in outside investors."

Raising money to finance production is often a producer's hardest task. The majority of works that are optioned are never produced. This is sometimes because script revisions are unsatisfactory or a collaboration between lyricist, librettist, and composer doesn't work. But more often, scheduled plays and musicals do not happen because the producer cannot raise the needed funds.

Producers use a variety of methods to raise money for their shows. Frequently, entertainment corporations such as movie and record companies put up a large proportion of the necessary funds. However, producers still look for individual investors. Backers' auditions, gatherings in which selections from the proposed show are performed and the producers describe their plans, are held to entice potential investors. Newspaper ads are placed in publications such as *The New York Times* and *The Wall Street Journal*, with the hope of attracting potential investors. However, the general feeling these days is that when a producer places such an ad, it is an indication that the project has been turned down by the corporations and theater owners, usually the Shuberts or Nederlanders, who frequently invest in shows other than their own. Some producers, of course, especially those few with consistently good track records in returning profits to their investors, do maintain steady investors who finance their shows. Gottlieb says, tongue in cheek:

"Anyone can be a producer. It's the only business I now where you can start at the top. You don't have to know how to read or write or count to ten. You don't have to have experience or talent. No license or degree is required, nor is any sense of honesty or honor. If you can separate fools from their money, you can be a producer."

The truth is, however, that good producing requires firsthand and detailed knowledge of the complex business of the theater. Gottlieb is known for his theatrical sensibilities, producing skill, and the care with which he spends his investors' funds.

"I'm the stingiest producer on Broadway, and that's why my shows make money. Too many producers are lavish with their investors' money, so they make the gossip columns but they don't make a profit.

"I have a group of about seventy-five people who put money into my shows. Some are wealthy and some are not. Some put in small amounts and some larger amounts. [Gottlieb's investors range from millionaires to Broadway stagehands and box office treasurers. He has a waiting list of those who want to invest in his shows.] I try not to have anybody put in a big sum because I like spreading it around. My investors come along from play to play, whether or not they think it's going to be a hit or a flop. They like to be part of the theatrical scene. I know all my investors personally. I used to say jokingly that I select my investors according to how good their cooks are."

Some of his plays, like *Tribute, Same Time, Next Year,* and *Sleuth* have made a lot of money. *Tribute,* which starred Jack Lemmon, paid back its investors the night it opened, an unprecedented Broadway event because it had such a successful pre-Broadway engagement. And like all producers, Gottlieb has had his share of flops, including *We Bombed in New Haven, Chips with Everything, Come Live with Me,* and his most recent and most expensive production, the 1982 season's *Special Occasions,* which opened and closed in one night at a loss of $750,000.

However, Gottlieb's record of hits, his reputation as a skilled and responsible producer, and his personal relationship with most of his investors has permitted him to present some plays that he felt were risky in terms of a successful commercial run but had artistic merit.

"For *Faith Healer,* which starred James Mason, a lot of my investors didn't feel they'd make money, and I didn't either. But we felt we had to do the play. It just had to be done. Under those circumstances I'll talk to the investors and say something like . . . 'Listen, who knows? Maybe we can work it out. Maybe we can get some good reviews. We've been able to set it up so it's not financially too high. We might be able to keep the show going, tour, and get our money out.'

"So the investors said that they would go along with it and take a chance that the play might become part of the heritage and literature of the Broadway theater. You see, a lot of my investors do come along with me on plays of certain distinction. They just feel that they want to be part of it all. I love it that way. We can't always expect to make a fortune on all the plays."

Like all producers, Gottlieb constantly receives scripts from playwrights and their agents. His office is piled with scripts: some read and rejected, some yet to be read, and some he simply won't read because "they're from agents I don't trust." Gottlieb does not produce many plays, perhaps one every few years. The plays that he chooses must relate to something within him.

"I do plays that I think I want to be part of at a particular time in my life. I want to devote a whole section of my life emotionally in terms of the time, energy, and everything else that one throws into a production. My tastes or my desire to work on something may vary from time to time, but I like the idea of doing a play for myself, hoping that the public and the press will appreciate it also. You do it as well as you can and as inexpensively as you can and you just hope that everything works out. I read many plays that I like and just don't feel like doing. I also read many plays that I would like to see but don't feel like devoting a portion of my life to. And I read many plays that I think might make money. But you can't sit back and say, 'Ah, this is going to make a fortune,' because the minute you do that, then that's the play that doesn't do well. It's a mistake to produce on the basis of what you guess the press and public are going to like."

Broadway producers must take costs into consideration when choosing plays. Obviously, musicals with multiple sets and large casts and backstage crews cost more to produce and run than smaller, one-set plays. Gottlieb produces plays, not musicals, and in addition to his subjective feeling upon reading a play, he is ultimately acutely conscious of the production's potential costs.

"You may decide to do a play for prestige only or transfer a production from some institutional theater. But you can't, on a commercial basis, find a way of staying alive with a play of say twenty-eight characters and do it from scratch. It's one thing if you see it done at a regional theater and bring it in. But we're talking about a costly show in terms of actors, stagehands, and dressers. You can't readily do it. But of course, every time you make a rule, it gets broken.

"Don't forget that if you had twenty actors getting scale at the time *Same Time, Next Year* was done, you would have been paying less than what Ellen Burstyn and Charles Grodin were getting, because they had percentages with guarantees against these percentages. So you can't always go with the numbers."

Once a producer selects a play, raises the money, and goes into preproduction (casting, negotiating for a theater, working with designers), he begins to oversee a large company. Although some producers act as their own general managers, most producers hire a general management office or, like Gottlieb, retain a general manager on staff. Ultimately responsible to the producer is a company that includes the general manager, press agent, director, designers, actors, advertising agency, ticket sales organization, and production workers. Most of these people have their own offices and staffs. One of the unique things about the business of the commercial theater is the extent to which many of its workers are individual entrepreneurs, working on several projects at once and maintaining their own offices and work spaces.

Today, most producers hire casting agents to fill the available roles in the production. Gottlieb, however, casts out of his own office. He retains a production stage manager on staff who, among other duties, coordinates and oversees the casting process.

"Sometimes how I respond to a script indicates to me how I would cast it. All those creative and administrative juices start flowing. As a matter of fact, I say to myself, 'Since all those juices are flowing, that is another sign that I should produce the play.'

"When it comes to casting, my production stage manager supervises the process, and it is done with the director and the author. Of course, I help with the decision. Agents often suggest people, but casting decisions come about in all sorts of ways.

"When we were casting for *Romantic Comedy*, Ben Rosenberg, my general manager, was looking through the *Players' Guide* and suggested Mia Farrow. I said, 'That's a very interesting idea, but has she done any stage work?' We called her agent and he got in touch with her. She read the script and said it sounded intriguing. Meanwhile, we found out that she had had more theater experience than almost any other star her age. She had done a lot of stage work. She came into town, we spoke, and she said that she would do the show. But the idea had come through Ben Rosenberg flipping through the *Players' Guide*.

"I'm very impressed with superstars. I love them and it excites me to deal with them. It's also easier to work with them than nonstars. Usually, the giant stars are more professional. They have the glamour but also the ability. They know what their job is. They are the ones who come to the theater earliest. For instance, Jack Lemmon is in his dressing room before the stagehands or even his dresser arrive at the theater.

"I think that the theater is larger than life. Therefore, actors should be larger than life. That's what going to the theater is about. It is about seeing an emotion expressed larger than life. And these big stars are larger than life. They give that extra dimension which is what the theater is. Theater is not small."

Gottlieb has worked with some of the entertainment world's biggest stars, including Jack Lemmon in *Tribute*, Mia Farrow and Anthony Perkins in *Romantic Comedy*, Ellen Burstyn and Carol Burnett in different companies of *Same Time, Next Year*, and Marlon Brando in what has turned out to be his last stage appearance in Shaw's *Arms and the Man*.

Once the casting is complete and the theater lined up, the play becomes a reality. Rehearsals begin and the producer is totally involved with the myriad details of production.

"I don't go to rehearsals after the first day. I try to stay away until the director says, 'Come around.' The director and actors are experimenting, and what they don't want is the producer checking up. What they are doing one day is not what they will be doing the next. So I drop in before rehearsals begin in the morning, at the end of the day, or even have lunch with people involved.

"I am constantly involved with all those technical details. How can we cut a couple of thousand dollars off the cost of the set; advertising; promotion; box office advance; should we go out of town . . .

"I prefer to go out of town. I think that if you do, everyone is in a pressure cooker, away from friends, relatives, and concerns. You go from the theater to the hotel and back to the theater. You eat your heart out, you're suicidal, and all the creative juices are going towards what's on the stage.

"Hopefully, you do some business out of town. [Many shows no longer preview out of town simply because of economics. It is rare for a show to make a profit out of town before its Broadway opening and most shows simply cannot afford to budget the extra money to support an out-of-town pre-Broadway run.] Going out of town and not doing business

is psychologically disruptive for everyone, especially the producer. Even actors are nervous about not doing business and
not having audiences. And you have all these decisions, such
as whether or not to paper [the practice of giving out free
tickets]. You don't want to paper too much because you might
end up losing potential sales. But you can't do a play without
an audience. It's very nerve-racking if you don't have some
kind of advance sale for a play that is coming up. Of course, if
you do too well, you can get smug. That's a danger. You can
almost sit back too much and say, 'Ah, it's working . . . don't
do anything more.' "

Then there's always opening night. Depending upon the
reviews, the show will run, close, or be what Gottlieb calls "a
nervous hit."

"The producer's job really begins the day after opening. If
it's a smash hit, then you try to figure out how you can make it
run a year longer. When I get a play that's very successful, I
milk it, starting right away.

"If it's a nervous hit, which I've had with some plays like
The Killing of Sister George, you try to figure out how to
tighten the belt. You have to identify your market, figure out
how to reach it, and think about how you're going to keep the
show going in February when there are snowstorms.

"If the show is a sure instant flop, you try to figure out how
to close the play quickly in order to save the investors'
money. You don't want to dribble away money keeping a play
around just to keep it going indefinitely. You're just taking
their investment, knowing that you can never get it back.

"Sometimes, though, you're wrong. *Faith Healer* is an ex-
ample. We didn't get a good review from the daily *New York
Times*, which was what we needed. But we got raves from
Newsweek, *The New Yorker*, and Walter Kerr in the Sunday

Times. And they were giant raves, recognizing the very unusual dramatic quality in the writing. But it was too late. We needed that stamp of approval right away from the *Times.* It could never have been a smash hit or a giant hit, but we thought we could do it. The Shuberts (who owned the theater) took no money; everybody took cuts in their royalties; and James Mason took a big pay cut. We all believed in the play but we couldn't keep it going."

After a play opens and the decision is made whether to close it or go for a run, advertising and publicity become important ticket-selling and audience-building tools. In the last decade, Broadway has started to utilize television as a medium for advertising, although the general consensus is that television is most effective for musicals and not ordinarily cost effective for plays.

"I believe that one of the real functions of a producer is to package and market. You must have a point of view about what is up on the stage and how to reach your potential audience. I don't believe that television commercials really pay off enough for plays. You have to spend too much money [producing them and buying the television time over which they are aired]. I believe in trying to get a lot of publicity."

One of Gottlieb's more flamboyant publicity stunts occurred after Sandy Dennis joined the cast of *Same Time, Next Year,* replacing Ellen Burstyn. A cat lover, at times Dennis has had over twenty-five cats at her Connecticut home. Working with his press agent, Gottlieb conducted a cat auction in front of the theater before a Wednesday matinee.

The most important thing though, Gottlieb believes, is word of mouth. Unlike some producers, Gottlieb constantly monitors his productions, making sure that energy and excitement remain high.

"I believe in keeping the performances so sparkling that the audience runs out and says to their friends, 'You've got to see this show.' "

The Not-for-Profit Artistic Director

In referring to the not-for-profit, regional theater, the word "revolution" is frequently used to describe what happened throughout the nation during the middle sixties. For it was during those years that the majority of the more than 160 resident producing organizations in approximately 85 cities and towns were founded.

The regional theater movement was based upon the premise that theater is a service institution and not a profit-making venture. The theaters defined themselves as community and educational resources; as environments for nurturing and developing new playwrights; as forums for experimental and nontraditional works; and as places for ensembles of resident actors and artistic personnel.

The theaters were formed in the tradition of such enduring institutions as London's Old Vic (1912), the Moscow Art Theater (1898), and such innovative, but short-lived United States producing organizations as the Provincetown Players and Eva Le Gallienne's Civic Repertory Company. The resident theaters were created under the spiritual guidance of Margo Jones, a woman from Dallas, Texas, who developed a plan for a permanent, professional repertory theater in the early 1940s. Her Dallas theater, established in 1947, and her book, *Theatre-in-the-Round*, published in 1951, embodied her dream, both practically and conceptually, of what became the regional theater movement in the United States. Although Margo Jones died in 1955, her vision and work formed the basis for the theater revolution of the 1960s.

Concurrently, in 1965, the federal government created the National Endowment for the Arts. By making direct monetary grants to arts organizations and funding state arts councils, the government helped nurture many of these newly created theaters. Foundations, in particular the Ford Foundation, made substantial contributions to many theaters, supporting production and the development of adjunct programs and activities.

New types of jobs were created because these theaters required the services of a professional staff. Managers, finance officers, development and audience-building specialists, resident designers, and technical experts are members of the permanent staffs of regional theaters. Many of the recent undergraduate and graduate degree programs in theater administration were created with the intention of providing trained personnel to assume these positions.

Today, government support for the theater is on the wane. Foundations, responding to changes in the public interest, are not as generous with grants to the theater. Despite this, the regional theater movement remains strong. Audiences support local theaters through subscriptions, ticket sales, special events, and volunteer work. There is a generation of knowledgeable theater professionals who direct and manage these theaters. Many theaters that suffered through growing pains, including haphazard management, internal strife, and conflict between governing boards and the theater management, have settled down to become harmonious, solvent, professional producing organizations. However, freedom from financial worries is practically unheard of. Nobody gets rich in regional theater, and fund raising is always among a theater's most pressing priorities.

Regional theaters are structured as year-round producing organizations. They have actors, directors, administrators, and designers who work together to present plays. They offer outreach programs to their communities. Unlike the commercial theater in which plays are presented on an individual basis with staff hired for each production, in regional theater each play is presented for a limited run as part of the theater's annual production season. Some theaters even employ a company of actors on a seasonal basis who perform in all or most of the theater's productions.

A not-for-profit regional theather has a board of directors, which is its governing body. The board is usually composed of members of the community who are either financially or socially well connected. The board has the mandate to help sustain the theater financially and provide the link between the theater and its community.

The key person in a regional theater is its artistic director. In the early stages of the movement, many of the artistic directors created and held together these developing theaters under great personal and financial adversity. Literally pioneers in an often turbulent process of development, many of the nation's most prestigious and successful regional theaters are still linked with their founding artistic directors, such as William Ball and San Francisco's American Conservatory Theatre, Gordon Davidson and Los Angeles's Mark Taper Forum, and Adrian Hall and Providence's Trinity Square Repertory Company.

The artistic director determines the course of the theater. It is a reflection of his interests, taste, sensibilities, and vision. Artistic directors work with managing directors who implement programs, oversee the day-to-day management, and work with the theater's board. The artistic director chooses the plays to be presented; selects actors, designers, and guest directors; and supervises all of the creative elements necessary for the production of the theater's plays.

Adrian Hall is founder and artistic director of the Trinity Square Repertory Company in Providence, Rhode Island.

*   *   *

"I could be called an absolute product of the repertory movement. I grew up in Texas where I worked with Margo Jones, one of the pioneers of the whole movement."

After teaching and working in the theater in Galveston, Hall served in the army during the Korean War. There he created the Seventh Army Repertory Theater, returning to Texas after the war. In the 1950s he came to New York, supporting himself by working in the box offices of various off-Broadway theaters and with occasional acting and directing jobs.

It was Hall's direction of Tennessee Williams's *Orpheus Descending* that established him, and for a while he moved back and forth between the commercial theater and the newly developing off-Broadway sector. Ultimately, Hall decided to reject the commercial theater, a decision that came just as the rumblings of the regional theater movement were first being heard.

"I'd never been anyplace where you got reviews and, overnight, people knew your name. That was wonderful, until I realized what a price one paid. Suddenly, people were fighting about the size of their names in the program. I was not interested in that, but I guess you've got to be interested if you're going to stay in the commercial world.

"I think that theater people knew for a long time that there had to be a revolution. If theater is dependent upon what five or six men write in a newspaper, using standards that nobody understands, it's obviously not a healthy situation. We had to break away from this highly centralized commercial world that is totally controlled by real estate and finances. We had to see if we could get away once and for all from the Shuberts and the Nederlanders, whose goals are so entirely different from ours.

"Our revolution was to build and create an indigenous American theater. We had to reclaim the theater for the people. Those first years were really wild. It was wide open. You could have gone anyplace and established a theater. There was a lot of turbulence in the beginning. Very few of us survived in the same geographic situation."

Hall was invited to Providence and came in 1964 with the proviso that he could bring a group of professional actors and start an acting company. He wanted to make it possible for actors to support themselves while having an ongoing life in the theater. He also set out to create a theater that would become "part of people's lives." The theater was to represent New England and the community in which it was situated.

For the first two years, Trinity Rep barely survived. Without a theater of its own, the company used performing spaces in the basement of Trinity Church, at the Albee Theatre, and later at the Rhode Island School of Design.

Then in 1966, Trinity Rep's third year of existence, the theater was the recipient of a grant from the National Endowment of the Arts and the United States Office of Education. Called Project Discovery, the three-year, $535,000 grant provided funds for the creation of productions and programs that would enable high school students to see and be exposed to theater. Every high school student in the state of Rhode Island was bussed to Trinity Rep four times a year. The grant gave Trinity Rep the means to develop and produce a season of plays and to begin functioning as a real theater company. At first, however, the grant was a mixed blessing.

"If you think that groundlings [those who stood in the theater's pit] in Shakespeare's time were rowdy, you should go out to the high schools in this country. We'd bring a thousand students to the theater every morning and they'd cut the seats and break the mirrors.

"We started out doing the accepted classics—*St. Joan, Ah Wilderness!, A Midsummer Night's Dream,* and *Three Sisters.* If you do Shakespeare, that's enough for the educational establishment. But we were having trouble with the kids. They were bored out of their little minds with that traditional so-called serious work. And we just didn't seem to be able to deal with the problem. You wouldn't believe our discussions in the early days. They were about things like should the kids wear a coat and tie when they came to the theater.

"By the end of the first season, thousands of students had come to the theater, but I really couldn't see that we were winning. I decided that it was now or never. We gradually began to shape the material and the company in an innovative kind of way. People began to note the kinds of things that were happening."

With resident designer Eugene Lee and composer-in-residence Richard Cumming, Hall decided to use the space between audience and actors differently. They redesigned the theater, abandoning the traditional proscenium stage. Instead, the stage was extended into the orchestra and bleechers were placed in various parts of the hall. In one of the first productions in the new space, a stage adaptation of Herman Melville's book *Billy Budd,* Hall staged an actual sea battle with water flying all over the house, cannons firing, and sailors climbing around the audience.

"The kids were totally mesmerized, almost exhausted by

the end of the first act. Then, when it came to the heavier moralizing in the second act, they were really ready to listen, just totally caught up in it."

Over the next few years, reflecting the turbulent and political 1960s, Hall cocreated and directed some startlingly innovative and controversial works. *Wilson in the Promised Land* was about hippies standing in judgment of six presidents; *Son of Man and the Family* was about Charles Manson; and *Years of the Locust* was about the imprisonment of Oscar Wilde. Trinity Rep was invited to take *Years of the Locust* to the Edinburgh Festival in 1968, marking the first time an American regional theater had ever been represented at the prestigious festival. In 1969 the theater received the first annual Margo Jones Award for production of new American plays. Trinity Rep was receiving critical attention and national publicity, and its audience was growing.

In 1971 Trinity Rep purchased the Shubert Majestic Theater, a downtown Providence movie palace that had once been a vaudeville house. It was purchased at a time when Providence's downtown area, like that of so many other cities, was decaying as people moved to the outlying suburbs. Trinity Rep gutted the building, with the exception of its marble and stained-glass lobby areas, and built two theaters, shops, rehearsal hall, and administrative offices.

"We became the flagship in the turnaround of downtown Providence's economy. I started to mix in more traditional fare with our experimental work, and our attendance increased dramatically."

Then, in 1975, the theater's board of directors decided to fire Hall. Ostensibly, the reason was the theater's deficit.

"We had a great upheaval. During the mad years of the movement in the 1960s, the big thing was to get anyone who was interested in theater to join the board. We ended up with a lot of people who weren't the movers and shakers of the community.

"What a board should do for an American theater is to keep the institution afloat. Like everything else, a theater will have its ups and downs. It must have support. You need people who can do more than just like theater.

"By the early 1970s, this group, which had been so anxious to be part of all the excitement, began to feel that they could dictate policy. They couldn't. One of the things I learned years ago is that a board cannot set artistic policy."

What had really upset the board, though, was Hall's experimental and controversial productions. Stating that Hall's personality and the "outlandishness" of his productions eroded community support and therefore made it impossible to raise money, the board decided to fire him.

"I knew I had something with this company. There was an ensemble and I wasn't going to let it go. I made a move that has been called crazy, but it worked. I said to the board, 'I fire you,' and refused to budge. And what happened was that the artistic community in this country really rallied. Actors took to the streets, television and radio got involved, newspapers in Boston and Providence began to support me, and telegrams poured in from all over. Each day, I really did think that I would be blocked from the theater, but it didn't happen. By the end of the summer, everyone was looking for a compromise."

The issue was finally resolved when Trinity Rep and the Foundation (its governing body) split. The Foundation retained the physical plant and divested itself of the responsibility of raising money for the company's operation. Hall formed his own board of directors and leased the theater from the Foundation for one dollar a year. Trinity Rep was the tenant and the Foundation the landlord.

This was not a unique situation, although Hall's ability to muster the kind of support he did and retain his position was. Throughout the regional theater movement, governing boards and artistic directors have clashed. The boards had always succeeded in ousting the artistic directors.

Most of the theaters survived, and of those Trinity Rep has become one of the most respected and successful regional theaters in the nation. In 1981 it was awarded a special Tony Award for its achievements.

"During the early 1970s, it was very difficult for an artist to stand up to a board. The screws were being put on artists, and usually by people who didn't have the foggiest idea what they were doing. It was just 'we don't want nudity in our community,' and that kind of nonsense.

"And, if it wasn't that, there was always that issue of fiscal responsibility. I think that a lot of our new image in town these days has to do with our finance committee chairman. Before, the banks wouldn't listen to us because they didn't respect us. Now, they listen because our chairman is on the board of the bank.

"Those years were tough, though. We were running an enormous deficit. But finally, things began to open up for us. Today, we have a board that raises the amount of money we need and is very supportive. We have over sixteen thousand subscribers. Over half our budget is earned through box office sales and the rest of our operational expenses has to come from private donations, endowments, and grants. Our staff can be as high as eighty-five actors and technicians."

Trinity Rep produces about twelve shows a year. The company tours frequently throughout the United States and has been sent by the State Department to India, Syria, and Egypt. Hall directs many of the productions himself, hiring directors for those he chooses not to direct. His adaptations of novels by John Steinbeck, Edith Wharton, and Herman Melville; his work with contemporary American playwrights such as Israel Horovitz and John Guare; and his collaboration with composer Richard Cumming and local writers have made Trinity Rep a truly American theater which at the same time reflects the spirit of its New England community.

"I believe that somehow our material has got to speak to the community and the company. Ours is a very sophisticated audience. We have been able to get John Guare, Harold Pinter, and Robert Penn Warren actually to come to this theater and participate in the rehearsal process. There is a real sense of it being a very special place.

"I have readers and people who really look for material both in Europe and New York. Sometimes, I'll get a call from London saying, 'Here is a play that we think Trinity would be interested in. We don't think it's going to have a commercial run. Would you like to read it?'

"There are some very good plays that are of no interest to us. For instance, the angry young man plays out of England in the 1950s. There's no way that they relate to Providence. We do a lot from the American past—Kaufman and Hart, Odets, and O'Neill. And, if given a choice, we would do a Sam Shepard play before one by Tom Stoppard, because Sam is an American writer.

"The choice also depends upon who is available. Some of our actors come back and forth. About eighty percent of the company has been together at least five years. In order to hold on to these fine actors, we have to let them go if they get a movie or television series. Katherine Helmond went off to do the television series 'Soap' and Ford Rainy, a wonderful actor, does films. Two years ago, he was available and the play *On Golden Pond* was available. We did it because it was a wonderful play for him, although we couldn't go more commercial than that show.

"If there has been a major change in the repertory theater movement, it has been in the thinking about the resident company. A lot of managements have realized that it's much more economical to use actors when you need them and then to let them go. But that's no way to have a company. It may be more efficient, but artistically it's not rewarding. Actors want to believe that if they are going to commit themselves to a life in the arts, they can survive.

"The difference between working in an institutional setting and the commercial theater is stunning. People don't really understand. They're always saying, 'Don't you want to come to Broadway? Isn't everyone's goal to be on Broadway?' If Broadway wants to use something of ours, that's fine. [In 1982, the Trinity Rep production of Harold Pinter's *Hothouse* moved to Broadway.] But it's hard not to fall right into that myth of the commercial world, where one night you're nobody and the next day they've hung a star on your dressing room. But we're an alternative to Broadway. We're not-for-profit; we're an ensemble; and we continuously work together.

"Basically, I do it all. I'm very demanding. There's nothing ever produced at Trinity that I haven't read myself. I try to evolve certain kinds of standards and philosophies on everything from graphics to the kinds of things that are written about us.

"One of the things that I find I must do over and over is define who we are. We are continually devising ways to tell people how they can relate to us. For instance, in an area where there is a college or university on every corner, we have to say, 'We're a resource. Why don't you use us?' For

Project Discovery and school children, we say, 'Why don't you bring students to see this experimental play instead of Shakespeare?'

"We also have to find audiences. There are a lot of people who want to contribute and relate to the theater but don't want to make telephone calls, ring doorbells, or do those volunteer-type things. We've created the Friends of Trinity Rep, which now numbers about sixteen hundred families."

These management and artistic responsibilities are, at times, incompatible with one another. Artists create and managers control. And there is always the proverbial "I just need five minutes of your time." To protect himself, particularly when he is in production, Hall makes sure that such business is funneled through his key staff members. "It's almost impossible to see me. If I allowed it to, making appearances and speeches would just take over my life."

Trinity Rep suffered, as most regional theaters have at some point in their operating histories, a period of shaky and changing management. Now, with a managing director who handles day-to-day management and the board of directors; a director of development who supervises press, audience development, and fund raising; and a production stage manager who oversees and coordinates the technical work on each production, Trinity Rep operates smoothly and consistently, carrying out the policies defined and set by Hall.

Theatrical Managers

The theatrical manager supervises all of the nonartistic parts of production. In the commercial theater, the title is general manager. In the not-for-profit theater, the title is usually managing director. For either though, the task is the same: to make the project run as smoothly, efficiently, and economically as possible. This is true whether it is a single Broadway play or the season's activities of a regional theater.

Commercial Theater

General Manager
The general manager is hired by the producer, usually as soon as the producer acquires a property. General managers have their own offices, although the few commercial producers who do maintain offices frequently retain a permanent general manager on staff.

General managers prepare the capitalization budget (the breakdown of monies required simply to open the show) and the operating budget (the sum required to run the show each week). They negotiate all contracts which, especially on Broadway, can get complicated. In addition to salaries and fees, those who work in shows often get royalties, which are a fixed percentage of a show's weekly income. In addition, billing (where and in what size a name appears in advertisements, in front of the theater, and on any other printed material concerning the show) and special provisions such as transportation to and from the theater for a star or individual dressing rooms are all part of contract negotiation.

Bid sessions, in which costume and set construction shops give estimates, take place in the general manager's office. The general manager negotiates the lease for the theater and usually offers advice about which theater to choose. On Broadway some theaters are better than others for certain shows. This is in part due to size and location, but also because of the various union rules that vary from theater to theater. For instance, certain theaters have agreements with the American Federation of Musicians, Local 802, which require a minimum number of musicians to be paid whether or not these musicians are in fact required for the show. Obviously, a production needing only nine musicians tries to avoid being housed in a theater where fifteen musicians must be paid each week, even if the theater is otherwise perfect for the show.

The general manager charges a fee for work done before opening. After the show opens, he gets a weekly sum for the duration of the production's run. Increasingly, general managers receive billing. Most general managers started out as company managers, the logical entry position to general manager.

Company Manager
In the commercial theater, the company manager is employed by the general manager to work on a single production. He is management's business representative at the

theater. Every show has a company manager who works out of the general manager's office and is at the theater for each performance, remaining until the box office closes and the box office statement has been signed.

The company manager handles the production's day-to-day business affairs. This includes the company payroll, union pension and welfare statements, supplies, and the production's bills. As the eyes and ears of the producer, the company manager is often in a position to anticipate potential problems.

On the road, the company manager often secures housing at special rates for the production's cast and crew (although this is also done by the advance agent or even the stage manager). He also supervises all the business and financial affairs of the traveling show.

The company manager must be a member of the Association of Theatrical Press Agents and Managers (ATPAM), the union for managers and press agents in the commercial theater. The company manager signs an ATPAM contract when hired to manage a show. Although general managers do not have to be ATPAM members, most are. Some even sign the union contract and act as company manager.

There are only about 250 manager members of ATPAM. Approximately 15 to 20 manager apprentices are accepted by the union each year. Apprentices are sponsored by general managers and must work under a general manager's supervision for two years. They must participate in a series of seminars that are organized jointly by the League of New York Theatres and Producers and ATPAM, and must successfully complete a written exam. It is not uncommon for aspiring company managers to work as low paid "go-fers" for several years before being proposed for union membership.

House Manager

All theaters have someone who is responsible for maintaining the building in which the show can play. On Broadway the house manager is a member of ATPAM and must satisfy the same entrance requirements as the company manager.

The house manager is employed by the theater owner. On Broadway most managers work for the Shubert Organization, which owns sixteen theaters, or for the Nederlander Organization, which owns ten. Managers are signed to contracts from Labor Day through the following Labor Day but actually work and receive salaries only when a show is in the theater.

Each theater has its own house staff of box office treasurers, mail order personnel, stagehands, ushers, cleaners, and engineers. The house manager is the person responsible for the theater's payroll and the disbursement of box office receipts to the production company whose show is housed in the theater.

The house manager oversees the maintenance of the theater, including dressing rooms, backstage areas, lavatories, and the entire auditorium area. He supervises the house employees and is responsible for the theater's security. He is at every performance and handles any problems that might arise with the audience, such as lost tickets, a physician who must be paged in the middle of a performance, or a sudden illness on the part of a theatergoer.

Peter Kulok is a partner in the general management office of Joseph Harris & Associates.

* * *

"I grew up very traditionally on Long Island and attended Boston University, entering as a business administration major. I was a good student, but after studying business administration I knew it wasn't for me and transferred to the School of Public Communications. It was more interesting and challenging, but since I was paying for school myself, I thought I should be more involved than I was. I was disenchanted and didn't know what I wanted to do.

"Through a friend, I heard about a job at the Westbury Music Fair as an apprentice stagehand. It was the only non-union position there and I had no idea what the job involved. But it was the perfect excuse for leaving school.

"I worked seven days a week for an average of about a hundred and twenty hours a week. We did a show every week. The show would close on Saturday night and we would immediately start the takeout [the dismantling of the sets, lights, and other equipment used for a production], which usually turned into an all-night proposition. I'd have a couple of hours off on Sunday morning, then Sunday afternoon the load-in [the setting up of all the scenery and equipment for a production] for the new show would start. On Monday night the show would open. However, the first time I heard the applause and realized that I had had something to do with them, I knew that the bug had hit. I was so high that I couldn't sleep and I still feel that way.

"After I had been at Westbury for about six weeks, the producers asked me if I would be resident stage manager. I went from being the crew's apprentice to being their boss. Half the crew were wonderful and the other half did everything they could to make me look bad. It was hard, but I lasted ten months and then decided it was time to move on.

"During that season, *No, No, Nanette* had played Westbury. I had met the producer and he hired me as show tech for the production, which was going on the summer stock circuit for four months. [The show tech is in charge of physically mounting and then dismantling a production.] Well, I immediately understood that there is a big difference between knowing something and doing it yourself. At Westbury I had a union crew and I had learned what had to be done to mount a show. On *No, No, Nanette* I had to coordinate everything myself. We would play one theater for a week or, if we were lucky, for two weeks. Sometimes we played theaters and sometimes tents. I drove a twenty-four-foot truck, unloaded it, and set up the entire show in a day. The only help I got was from each theater's apprentices who were, more often than not, teenagers paying to learn about the theater. I never stopped. I often went three nights without sleep. But I never learned more about the theater, people, or myself in any period of my life.

"I was paid a hundred fifty dollars a week, and out of that I had to pay all of my own expenses. I often wanted to leave, but I knew that there were at least twenty other people who would take that job in a minute. I knew that I was good, but I also knew that the producers didn't care about good, better, or best. One of the truths about the theater is that a job can get done well or badly, but basically people just want it done. You don't have that much leverage.

"When the tour was over, I came to New York thinking I was a real hotshot. I had decided that I wanted to be a stage manager. I wasn't in the union [stage managers in the theater are members of the actors' union, Actors' Equity] and I didn't really understand how important the union was. I just went around and spoke to everyone I could. I got in to see general managers and a couple of stage managers. People were very nice but it was basically the Catch-22 position: I had no experience as a stage manager but no one would give me a job to give me experience.

"I finally got a job in the office of a Broadway producer. I was still making only a hundred fifty a week, but at least I wasn't on the road. I did a lot of the nuts-and-bolts work on his shows and assisted the company managers on each of the shows. I learned a lot about how the business works during the year I was there. But the shows closed and since I had been the last hired, I was the first to be let go. I got a job with a general manager who worked on off-Broadway shows most of the time and handled some theater-related businesses from his office.

"I ran the office for two years. It was not a happy time for me. I was desperately trying to get my apprenticeship with the union as a manager. It's never easy to get into ATPAM, and the person for whom I was working didn't have very good relations with the union at that time. Finally, after the third year, I was accepted as an apprentice.

"While I was working on one of this manager's projects, I met Joe Harris and Ira Bernstein [two of the busiest general managers in the commercial theater]. I knew their reputations and really liked them. One day, I just blurted out . . . 'Ira, I'd really like to work with you someday.' He was very kind and said he had nothing, but would remember me when he did. And of course, I believed him. Now that I'm in that position myself, I know he heard that every day.

"What really seemed to do the trick, though, was a chance meeting at Cape Cod's Melody Tent. I was taking my first vacation in over four years and met Ira at the Melody Tent. He invited me for a drink and we spent some time together. When I got back to my office the next Monday, the phone rang. It was Ira offering me a job. I really think that it was this chance meeting that did the trick. It's like so much in this business—luck, chance, whatever—but when it happens, it's great.

But it was very hard work. The office was managing *The*

Act starring Liza Minnelli. I had been working off-Broadway for a long time and was very comfortable there. But here I was acting as a company manager and dealing with a big star, star dressers, a Broadway box office, and Broadway stagehands. It was like being thrown to the wolves. But I kept thinking back to my Westbury days and managed to appear confident even when I was shaking inside. And I learned. And I became a company manager."

Kulok worked as a company manager with Harris/Bernstein for five years. He worked in New York and on the road handling shows including *Chicago, On the 20th Century, Groucho, Pippin,* and *Sophisticated Ladies.* When Ira Bernstein moved to California the firm became Joseph Harris & Associates, and Kulok became a partner and general manager.

Traditionally, general managers act on behalf of the producer and manage the nonartistic parts of production. When there were many active producers on Broadway who maintained ongoing offices, most had a general manager on staff who managed the offices' shows. They prepared budgets and contracts with actors and artistic personnel, set up bid sessions at which prices for sets and costumes were presented by the construction shops, worked with lawyers, accountants, and insurance personnel, set up and supervised the box office at the theater, and oversaw all the production's financial matters.

Today, many producers have never worked in the theater and depend upon the general manager literally to guide them in their role as producer. Union regulations, contract negotiations, scheduling, and even deciding when to open the show involve complicated decisions calling for the experience, familiarity, and subtle understanding available only to an experienced theater professional.

"The business has changed over the last decade. Today's producers are often neophytes in the theater. They either have a lot of money or a good script—sometimes both—but most of the people we see today are first-time producers. This means that my position as general manager becomes the equivalent of say, a line producer in television or film. We actually produce the show for a lot of these people.

"Assuming funds for production are available, a producer ideally comes to us four to six months before the day of the first rehearsal. The first thing we do is prepare the capitalization and operating budgets. We look at the script and talk to the producers and/or director about their ideas for the show. We have to know the size of the cast; how big and how complicated the set will be; whether they are planning an out-of-town tryout; if there is going to be a television commercial in advance of opening; if it is a musical, what size orchestra is planned. On the basis of answering these questions, the budget is prepared. Plans are frequently revised in order to accommodate available funds or those that can be raised.

"We also make recommendations about creative personnel for the show. For instance, some designers are very budget conscious and work well within budgetary limitations. Others do wonderful work but are unconcerned about budgets. We suggest designers based on the show's budgetary capabilities.

"We often suggest the time the show should open. If it is an 'iffy' show, meaning that there isn't a big star with box office appeal, you want to open at a time when shows traditionally do well, such as the beginning of fall or early spring. And we negotiate all the contracts."

Contract negotiation is one of the manager's most sensitive tasks. Contracts, particularly with a big star, do not just involve salary or fee. They include royalty payments, billing, house seats [prime location seats that are sold to selected individuals], limousine transportation to and from the theater, exclusive dresser and hairdresser, right of first refusal to do subsequent companies in the same role, options on renewing contracts, and dressing room decoration including television, telephone, and refrigerator. These extras often involve substantial costs and can mean the difference between a show that runs because it has managed to hold down expenses and a show that simply cannot break even and is forced to close because so many extras have been included in contracts.

"There's an art to negotiation. You have to learn where to be tough and where to compromise. People rarely get what they originally hoped for, but you don't want to be insulting by initially offering something too low. If you do that, they'll never settle for as low as they might have. The trick about negotiating is to break down barriers in communication. You must realize how people are responding to you and you better know how to make them respond favorably. I much prefer negotiating with agents than with the artists themselves. Agents usually have more of a business sense. When you're negotiating with the artist, you get so concerned about feelings that it's difficult to make certain important points. And of course, you don't want to start out with a difficult relationship. Whatever you go through with an agent, it is over the first day of rehearsal, and that's when you meet the artist for the first time."

General managers are also concerned with scheduling and coordination. Especially if a show is going out of town for a pre-Broadway tryout, the coordination and scheduling can become overwhelming. The general manager must make sure that sets and costumes are not only completed in time but arrive at the theater at the right time and in good shape. Lights and sound equipment that are leased must be delivered as well. Rehearsal space, rooms with pianos for musical preparation specialists and the composer, housing, and countless other details must be attended to.

"Basically you want to get everyone and everything on stage as soon as possible. It's mad and absolutely insane. It's simply nonstop all day and night. Each department and individual has problems and everyone comes to the manager for a solution. My main concern, though, is to schedule everyone's work around union rules in order to maximize efficiency of time. The last thing you want is to pay double and triple overtime to stage crew members who can't do anything but sit around and wait for people to finish work."

General managers often find themselves involved in artistic decisions. This frequently occurs when the show is in previews and decisions involving money must be made. It is here that the combination of business and theatrical experience is vital.

"We help with judgments. During previews, I watch the show at each performance. I look for audience reaction, how the technical aspects work, how the show looks, and whether the money spent shows where it should. We are constantly asked about changes. For instance, someone says that the choreography doesn't work. I might say, 'It's not the choreography but the clothes. Try pants instead of skirts.'

"Of course, it depends upon with whom you are working. If you're working with well-established theater people, you don't offer opinions unless you are asked. But less-established theater people ask regularly.

"Often you have to decide if you should go over budget. You have to be able to decide if it is worthwhile for the show. Sometimes, you get a situation where a song is just terrible and should be reorchestrated. I can tell the producer that it's going to cost five hundred dollars for the orchestrations, but that there won't be a chance for the show if it's not done.

Sometimes the designer wants to make a lighting change. It might involve a call for the entire crew and cost about twenty-five hundred dollars. You have to know whether the change is going to make much of a difference, because if it won't, you just don't spend the money.

"We have to know what is important and what isn't. I believe that our office has a theatrical feel. I can tell you what works and what doesn't work. I can't tell you how to fix a show, though. I can read an audience and its reactions and I can evaluate the consequences of a change. I can read blueprints and I'm there for bid sessions for sets and lights. I think it is invaluable for a manager to be aware of the technical end of theater. That way, if someone comes to me and says that something is necessary, I know what they are talking about and can offer alternatives and ideas. I regularly recommend money-saving shortcuts that won't affect the look of the show but do save time and money.

"Except when you're dealing with specific situations, such as union rules or basic accounting procedures, there are no rights or wrongs. So much of the theater is based upon judgment and there is simply no substitute for experience."

Not-for-Profit Theater

Managing Director

The managing director should possess the same business skills and theater sense as the commercial general manager. However, in regional and institutional theater the managing director must have strong administrative skills. The entire staff of the theater and all of its programs are under his direction. In the commercial theater the producers hire individuals on a per show basis. Those hired usually work out of their own offices. Regional theater, however, is an ongoing business with designers, promotion, marketing, financial, and maintainence staff all under the managing director's supervision.

Regional theaters are governed by boards of directors with whom the managing director works very closely. Increasingly, managing directors must also have fund-raising expertise. Although there is usually a development office that assumes the daily tasks involved in fund raising, such as the identification of funding sources and the preparation of grant proposals, the primary fund-raising responsibility often falls on the managing director. This is true particularly in smaller theaters which cannot afford the salary of a full-time professional development director. The managing director is often the theater's most visible member. He must act as the theater's spokesman in addition to generating long-range financial and fund-raising goals.

Managers in the not-for-profit theater do not have to be union members. Since there are more regional and institutional theaters than commercial productions, there are more employment opportunities regionally. A degree in theater management or arts administration is increasingly popular. However, opinions are mixed about the actual benefit of such degrees. There is general consensus that there is no substitute for practical experience, and even with a graduate degree, an aspiring manager is unlikely to be hired in an upper-level management position without first working in a middle-management position, such as finance or marketing.

Business Manager

Working under the managing director, the business manager supervises the theater's financial operation. He helps prepare budgets, pays the bills, oversees banking and accounting procedures, and handles the revenues received from box office sales, subscriptions, grants, and donations.

Company Manager
This is a nonunion position in the not-for-profit theater. Larger theaters that have several producing companies often assign each a company manager to oversee its day-to-day operations.

William Stewart is managing director of the Hartford Stage Company.

* * *

"I've been in the theater in one form or another since I was eleven years old. All through high school and college, I was an actor and director and occasionally a designer. I had assumed that I would work in the theater as an actor. But after I was married, had served in the army, and had a child, I decided that I was basically not equipped to do what an actor has to do. So I made the decision that I was not going to pursue an acting career in New York and would go to graduate school instead.

"I went to the University of Miami because, as an undergraduate at Knox College, I had been fortunate in working with a very fine man in its theater department. When he transferred to Miami to become chairman of the theater department, I left Knox and got my undergraduate degree from Miami. I was offered a scholarship and assistantship there for graduate work.

"It turned out to be very fortunate that I did go back to Miami, because one day I was told that the Ford Foundation was beginning a new program for administrative interns. Ford had put its first major money into the resident theaters in 1959. It had given major grants to some theater companies principally in the area of artist support, such as actors' salaries and play development. What Ford discovered, however, was that some very exciting work was being done, but there was no management structure at all. Something had to be done. This was in 1961, and at that point there were no college or university management programs for the arts or the theater.

"Ford decided to place a number of people as management interns with not-for-profit theaters, symphony orchestras, and opera companies. They expected to draw candidates from theater departments and business schools. I was interviewed and felt that, in all honesty, I couldn't say I would be a theater administrator. I had frankly assumed that I would teach in college. But the opportunity seemed good and I said that if I got the grant, I wanted to go to the most New York–oriented situation I could, since I had had no experience with professional theater, only community and educational theater.

"I was selected and placed with the American Shakespeare Festival in Stratford, Connecticut. It turned out to be an enormous opportunity. In retrospect, it cut out ten years of kicking around and sorting my life out. One of the things that I believe about internships in general is that they only work if you are real tenacious. You've got to make your own situation because no one will do that for you. Stratford turned out to be a fortunate choice for me because it was, as it has been since its founding, in a state of disorganization. There were great voids and vacuums and it was easy to look around and say, 'Aha! I'll do that.' "

At the end of the internship, Stewart was hired as assistant to the producer at Stratford and went on to become administrative director. He ran the school program, supervised publicity and advertising, and functioned as company manager. While at Stratford, Stewart began to understand the real distinction between not-for-profit institutions and the commercial theater.

In many ways, Stratford was set up as a combination of the two. It had a governing board of directors and a small, but permanent, administrative staff. Yet a commercial theater press agent and general manager were hired during its production season and its board was composed primarily of people with a commercial theater background. A weekly operating statement reported the profit and loss for each show rather than a monthly income and expense report for the entire institution, as is usual for not-for-profit, institutional theater. All this made for a rather difficult situation, and in 1967 Stewart moved to Cincinnati to become managing director of the Cincinnati Playhouse in the Park.

"When I went there, there was no staff except for the artistic director, me, and a woman who was essentially a bookkeeper. We had no box office staff, no front-of-house staff, and no publicity or marketing staff. I did everything. Today, I consult with a lot of developing theaters and my Cincinnati experience has turned out to be very helpful. I know that one person can do it all. But it was horrible. I was never home and it was rough. But I've been there and know that you can write a press release at two A.M., get it to the local newspaper in time for the Sunday paper deadline, and also run a box office at the same time."

In 1969 Stewart came to the Hartford Stage Company as managing director. Founded in 1964, Hartford produces six plays a year and has an annual operating budget of about $2 million. It occupies a $2.5 million complex that opened in 1977 and has a production and administrative staff of about forty-five who work on a seasonal (October through June) or year-round basis. Its artistic director is Mark Lamos, who assumed the position in 1980 after Paul Weidner, who had held the post since 1968, resigned to join the Peace Corps.

The majority of the nation's regional theaters are set up with a governing board of directors and administered by an artistic director and managing director who are hired by the board. The relationship between the artistic director and the managing director is crucial. Both must share a mutually complimentary view of the direction in which the theater should move, including its short- and long-term goals.

"We are a board-of-directors theater. This theater is here because the community wants it, and the board maintains the continuity of the theater. I am hired by the board and so is the artistic director. Neither of us works for the other. We work for the board.

"The artistic director is responsible for the artistic guidance of the theater as a whole. That includes the selection of the season, a company, and guest designers and directors. But most important, the artistic director provides the artistic thrust of the institution. The managing director's role is to provide the resources to make that work possible. Therefore, most of my work is administration and keeping the institution financially healthy, physically functioning properly, and providing the backup for Mark and the other artists."

Stewart has seen situations in which artistic director and managing director had totally divergent ideas about the theater's goals, creating an artistic, administrative, and financial shambles. One of the prerequisites in establishing a good working artistic director–managing director relationship, Stewart believes, is a practical theater background on the part of the managing director.

"I firmly believe that the final decision on any matter must rest with the artistic director. For instance, Mark sees all the brochures and subscription-campaign plans before they have been finalized, because they are statements about the institution. And the institution's statement must come from the artistic director.

"But I also believe that the best managers are people who have done the other side of the work. They must understand the decision-making process in the theater. I have very little enthusiasm for most of the arts-management programs in this country. A business-school program tends to be highly theoretical, offering very little practical experience. People come out expecting to make a high salary and to be placed right at the top. They are not prepared to go into middle-management positions like marketing or business. They want to be managing directors right away, and they're just not equipped. They have few of the people skills required and very little of the practical skills involved in what you do day to day.

"When Mark and I talk, I can bring a certain understanding to the decision-making process because of my theatrical background. If Mark says, 'I've got to have this costume no matter what the cost' or 'We really need a sound engineer for this show,' I can understand what he means and on what basis he feels it is necessary."

The managing director prepares the theater's annual budget, shepherding it through the various board committees on its way to passage. He negotiates contracts with actors, designers, and playwrights or their agents. He must also have strong administrative abilities, as he oversees the financial, development, audience-building, production, technical, and educational programs for the theater. In addition, Stewart, like most general managers, spends a large portion of his time working with the board of directors and its committees.

"You must have a very strong, mutually respectful relationship with your board of directors. Working with the board is a continual activity, and a lot of my time is spent at it. We have a large board; it's seventy-three people. People get hung up on how big a board should be. I feel it can be as large as can effectively function and do its job.

"I believe that a board functions best when the management has carefully identified the role that each member can play and makes appropriate use of each member. A healthy board is one that renews itself on a regular basis. Ideally, a board term should be two years and no one should stay more than three terms. You want to get people who are up and coming in the community on the board. Our board became very strong in 1968 when its then president went to the Hartford Chamber of Commerce and asked them to identify the people at each of the insurance companies and banks who would one day be president. We got them to join the board.

"Basically, we expect three things from our board members. First, each member should contribute financially to the institution. Some will contribute more than others, but a well-balanced board should have a good proportion of people who can make a substantial contribution. Second, members should have the ability to give us access to other sources of funds such as corporations and foundations. Third, the board should interpret us to the community and interpret the community to us. They are our antennae out there.

"A good board is structured with a consciousness of what the community and its outside resources are and how we can get to them. The board is divided into committees, including an executive committee, a nominating committee which identifies resources and possible new members, a development committee, a finance committee, a facilities committee, and an audience committee. Special committees are formed for specific needs, such as the search committee which identified candidates to replace Paul as artistic director.

"We always go to board meetings. Board members must never meet by themselves. In a very real sense, the job of the managing director is to tell the board of directors what it is to tell the managing director to do. Generally speaking, I should be at every committee and full board meeting. But I have a very strong staff and I've missed a few meetings of the facilities committee, which were covered by the general manager, and the audience committee, which were covered by the marketing director.

"I once wrote an article for *Theatre Crafts* titled 'Have You Called Your Board President This Week?' It's easy to sit here and ignore the board and just go about your work. The work is all-encompassing and the tendency is to think 'I don't need them because they don't know anything about theater.' But that's when you get into trouble. Actually, the best kind of board member is a person who has never been near a theater in his life but brings a sense of community, an understanding of fiscal matters, and a willingness to work. We have a model board here, but a board must be constantly educated and a lot of my time is spent doing just that."

Throughout the history of the regional theater movement, there have been conflicts between boards and theater staffs, particularly artistic directors and boards. Although a board of directors is the theater's governing arm, it does not make artistic decisions.

"The board has got to feel part of the decision-making process, but with a clear understanding that they don't have any say in the selection of plays. It's important, though, that they have access to the artistic director. It's very easy to become isolated and insulated from your community in an institution like this. This is particularly true for the artistic director, who frequently has very little community contact because of his working life-style. It is important to know how people are feeling about the institution and its work. This is a function for the board.

"However, you don't do plays based on what your audience supposedly wants. For instance, you don't sit around and say, 'Oh, they want Neil Simon, so we'll do Neil Simon.' But, because a theater is rooted in its community and exists because of the community, it has to be aware of a certain balance during a season. Mark discusses what he is doing with the board, but never with the notion of 'I'm asking you.' That must be totally understood by the board.

"And the bottom line, of course, is that they have the ability to hire and fire the artistic director and the managing director. If they don't like what Mark is doing, they can fire him. But they shouldn't tell him what to do. If they think I have become fiscally irresponsible and sloppy, they should get rid of me. They just shouldn't try to do my job."

Although the not-for-profit theater sector increasingly provides material for the commercial theater, Stewart does not see this as a conscious choice for Hartford.

"I have no interest in working in the commercial theater. I find that decisions are made only with regard to financial considerations and with very little concern for artistic sensibilities.

"We do new work and hope that it might have a further life in New York. But we don't get much from it when it does. [When a work is picked up from a regional theater and moved to the commercial theater, the originating theater gets a small royalty, usually only one or two percent.] We feel that the theater is an art form. That is what the not-for-profit theater was created to reestablish in this country, and that's what it should do."

Promoting Shows
and Theaters

One of the facts of life for all theater, whether commercial or not-for-profit, is that money doesn't magically appear. In the commercial theater, investors finance a particular show, but it will run only if an audience buys tickets. In the not-for-profit realm, paying audiences must supplement monetary grants to support the life and continuance of the producing organization.

All theater, therefore, needs people to act as liaisons between the theater and the outside world. Their function is to generate understanding, interest, and excitement in the theater or production. If successful, these efforts will create audiences and, for not-for-profit theater, the unearned income in the form of grants and contributions which is vital to the life of these institutions.

These positions come under the broad category of promotion. There are more career opportunities here in regional and institutional theater than in the commercial theater. In the commercial theater, the producer hires a press agent who is retained only for the run of the show. In the not-for-profit theater, there are year-round positions.

Not-for-Profit-Theater

Director of Development

Not-for-profit theaters depend upon foundation, government, corporate, and individual grants for a significant part of their revenues. The sources for this unearned income range from local community groups that are mobilized to hold fundraising events to national corporations and foundations that annually donate substantial sums of money to the arts. Government organizations, including the National Endowment for the Arts, and state and community arts councils also provide funding for not-for-profit theater.

The director of development identifies possible sources for grant monies, and researches and writes proposals for these funds. He organizes fund-raising events and parties and often works with volunteers from the theater's constituent community.

Marie Nugent-Head is executive director of the National Corporate Theatre Fund. Prior to that, she was director of development for the Pittsburgh Public Theater.

* * *

"I am originally from France and grew up in Paris. My first real job was as the assistant to an agent in Paris. I read British and American scripts to see whether they could be adapted to the French stage or for film. However, when I was about to be married, my fiancé, realizing that show business is not very compatible with marriage or its continuity, begged me to quit. I did, those being unliberated times, and started to raise a family."

Her husband's career caused the family to move frequently, resulting in a series of constantly changing jobs for Ms. Nugent-Head. In Seattle, Washington, she taught

French and Russian at the University of Washington and volunteered at the then newly founded Seattle Repertory Theatre. Her introduction to fund raising came when the family moved to Boston and she worked as a fund raiser for the Musician's Emergency Fund.

"When we moved to Pittsburgh in 1974, I decided to be very cautious about what I would do next. I had worked all my life, but every time we moved, I was yanked from a job and a commitment. So I decided that this time, whatever I ended up doing, it would have to be something that I could take with me wherever we ended up. I realized that fund-raising skills would probably be increasingly in demand. So I proceeded to look for a position.

"At that time, there was no theater in Pittsburgh. Ten years before, William Ball's American Conservatory Theatre had been there. But Pittsburgh wasn't ready for it, and the theater stayed for only one season. I had heard that there was a group trying to establish a regional theater and attended a press conference at which the formation of the new theater, the Pittsburgh Public Theater, was announced.

"Nothing really happened until about a year later, when a friend of mine interviewed for the position of director of development. The artistic director was putting together a staff and wisely had decided that one of the first positions to be filled was that of director of development. My friend didn't feel that she was right for the job and recommended me. I met with the artistic director and the president of the board, and the next week I started to work.

"Pittsburgh is the third largest corporate center in the United States. One of my advantages was that, although I was relatively new to the city, I was very well connected, particularly to the business community. One of the difficulties most development directors face when they join a new theater is that they don't know the community and the community doesn't know them. It takes time to establish credibility and it is something that you cannot short-cut.

"We realized that our fund-raising efforts would have to have a very strong business approach and were very fortunate that our artistic director had the rare quality of being both a gifted director and a savvy businessman.

"We were also willing to work very hard. The toll on all our private lives was high and, with the exception of me and the artistic director, everybody burned out within a few years. We worked twenty-four hours a day and functioned like machines. I probably had had the right instinct about thinking I shouldn't go back into theater. I don't regret it but I did pay a high price in terms of my family and marriage.

"We didn't ask for a single penny in the beginning. Instead, we did extensive research into every aspect of our fund-raising activities. We never made a move until we were really prepared and had done all our homework. Everything was done with an enormous amount of thought and follow-up. I think that there are three words which describe the key to effective fund raising: perfectionism, meticulousness, and thoroughness.

"One of the things that all development directors must do is make the board of directors look and feel good. We had a very good working board and were able to maintain a small staff because the board was willing and able to work so hard. They made introductions for us to the right corporate and foundation people. One of the things I learned is that, as a staff member, it is important to go one step behind your board members when dealing with the business community. No matter how well you might know key corporate people, peer-to-peer pressure is always better. One of the reasons people serve on the board is because of the access and entrée they can give you.

"We met with the major corporations based in Pittsburgh, including the Heinz Corporation, Gulf Oil, and U.S. Steel, and with foundations such as the A. W. Mellon Educational Fund, the Mellon Foundation, and the Ford Foundation. We really felt that Pittsburgh wanted the best and was willing and able to support it. After all, they have a flourishing symphony, ballet, and museum. But we also knew that Pittsburgh is a conservative town. We spent a lot of time explaining what kind of theater we were going to be; why we were different; and how we were going to be managed. In asking for money, it is essential to show good fiscal management."

Foundations, corporations, and government agencies always expect grant applicants to account for their past financial situations and project into the future. Currently, with support to the arts diminishing, sound financial management will probably be the determinative factor in the survival or demise of the smaller not-for-profit regional theaters.

"After all the groundwork was done, we started to develop proposals. Basically, a proposal means that you are asking for money. And, let's face it, there are only so many ways you can ask for money. Yet we were very careful in how we did this and always went through the same process.

"We spent a lot of time doing what I call 'massaging,' through our letters and proposals. One of the most tiring aspects of fund raising is that at least sixty percent of the time is spent grinding out letters and proposals. They must look good, read well, and be short and to the point. The higher the level at which you are dealing, the more respectful you must be of a person's time. Everything must be done in a businesslike and organized manner, especially in a place like

Pittsburgh. Perhaps some other cities are ready to celebrate the artistic entity and will allow you to get away with more of an artistic temperament, but not a place like Pittsburgh."

Although government agencies and foundations provide grants primarily on the basis of merit and the prevailing opinion about what most benefits the public, corporate grants are usually based in part on what the recipient can do for the corporation. A corporation expects to receive more than a tax deduction for its contributions. Sometimes public recognition of the corporation's good works will suffice, but on a local level, most corporations want something back in return.

"We knew, for instance, that the United States Steel Workers Union would feel that community outreach was important. So we stressed our public-school programs, inner-city training opportunities, and apprentice internships in our proposals to them. Especially now, with money so tight, many of the major corporations that have traditionally supported the arts are retrenching and rethinking their patterns of giving. Theaters must be perceived as offering programs as worthy as, say, 'meals on wheels' and other social services often supported by the corporate realm.

"We were fortunate in that the theater's staff complemented one another. The financial and public relations departments are vital to the development office's function. If you are going to be any good as a development director, you must be successful at dealing with the theater's entire staff. You can't go to the other offices in a rage and say, 'Your salary wouldn't get paid if it weren't for what I do.'

"When you present a proposal, you must back it up with the kind of information that is compiled and furnished by the financial and public relations offices. But you can't forget that they have their own jobs to do. You must be very respectful of the artistic and managing directors' time and priorities.

You might be doing a fund-raising telethon and want the artistic director to speak to all the volunteers. But perhaps he really needs to be at rehearsal during that time. You get torn and the impulse is to say to yourself, 'I worked my head off to get this whole thing together and he can't even give me five minutes!' You need everybody, but you are always making demands on people and everyone is usually under pressure."

Government agencies provide support to the arts. The federally supported National Endowment for the Arts gives grants as do state arts councils. Each state has an arts council and most cities and communities have organizations that also provide some funding. Although government support of the arts is certainly on the wane since its period of relative magnanimity in the late 1960s and early 1970s (and even then, the United States government played a very small role in supporting the arts when compared to other nations), government agencies do offer funds for theaters and various arts programs.

"We lobbied within the state and federal government. We wanted Pittsburgh to be perceived as a real arts center, since most state and federal grants went to programs in Philadelphia. We went to the National Endowment for the Arts in Washington, D.C., and to the Pennsylvania capital, Harrisburg. Again, we were thorough and anticipatory in all our actions.

"Even before we started applying for government grants, we began a low-key campaign. We inundated all our congressmen and federal and state senators with copies of our material and letters. We used our board members for introductions to the right people and for lobbying when necessary. We wanted to be noticed and even applied for an NEA grant a few months short of our qualification time. [Theaters are not eligible for NEA grants until they have been established and have been operating for at least two years.] Well, we didn't get it, but we certainly made an impression.

"We never lost sight of the fact that we were a public theater. That's why our name was the Pittsburgh Public Theater. We never publicized the names of donors in any special category like 'patron' or 'sponsor.' No one knew whether someone had given fifty cents or five thousand dollars. We kept our ticket prices low and they are still comparatively low for the regional circuit today. The number of people who continue to support the theater is extraordinary.

"The one area we did not handle well was our public campaign, which had been started by volunteers. There had originally been two women on the board who organized a volunteer program. Their husbands were relocated rather early in the theater's life, but before they left these women managed to organize over three hundred fifty volunteers. We didn't have the patience or know-how to nurture these volunteers and it cost us.

"Volunteers are needed on all levels, but particularly for subscription campaigns and fund-raising events. When we started the theater, it was at the time when many women were deciding that they no longer wanted to do volunteer work. Those who were willing to continue needed special attention and respect. You need a first-class volunteer organizer who is committed, intelligent, and has a good relationship with the board and theater staff. We didn't follow through well and it was too bad."

In 1979 Marie Nugent-Head decided the time had come to leave the Pittsburgh Public Theater. She gave a year's notice and then moved to New York City to become executive director of the National Corporate Theatre Fund, a not-for-profit corporation that develops financial support from major corporations for its eight member theaters: the Actor's Theatre of

Louisville, San Francisco's American Conservatory Theatre, Washington, D.C.'s Arena Stage, the Cleveland Playhouse, Chicago's Goodman Theatre, Minneapolis's Guthrie Theater, New Haven's Long Wharf Theatre, and the Seattle Repertory Theatre.

Each of the member theaters has its own director of development, who concentrates fund-raising efforts on foundations, governmental agencies, and local corporate and community groups. The eight member organizations of the National Corporate Theatre Fund are among the nation's most prestigious and longest-established regional theaters and must satisfy exacting criteria for membership, including nationally recognized artistic excellence, financial stability over a ten-year period, and the generating of at least fifty-five percent of their annual budget through earned income. They are assessed a monthly fee for their participation in the Fund.

When Marie Nugent-Head left the Pittsburgh Public Theater, it was operating with an annual budget of $2.2 million and had over 14,000 subscribers. The theater was supported by grants and contributions from 48 corporations, 27 foundations, and 2,800 individuals, as well as federal, state, and county agencies.

Director of Audience Development

The director of audience development concentrates on increasing the potential of earned income (money from ticket sales) for the theater. The position requires the identification and development of new audiences and devising ways to get these audiences into the theater. The director of audience development manages subscription campaigns that aim to get people to buy tickets for an entire season rather than on a per performance basis. The position requires an understanding of direct-mail techniques, the ability to write and oversee the design of subscription brochures, and, above all, creativity in seeking new strategies for increasing the theater's audience over the long term.

Director of Public Relations

The public relations representative of a theater handles all contacts between the theater and the media, which include radio, television, newspapers, and magazines. In addition, the public relations director coordinates and supervises any advertising of the theater's productions.

The goal of publicity is to present the theater, its programs, and productions in a favorable and enticing way to the public. The public relations director deals with critics who come to review productions and any press, radio, or television reporters who are interested in doing stories about the theater.

Obviously, it is important that the public relations office maintain good relationships with media representatives and understand their special needs. The position requires writing skills as all press releases, announcements, and theatrical programs emanate from the press office. Most important, though, is a publicity sense, which is acquired from experience. This enables an experienced public relations representative to develop good story and photo possibilities. He must then have the knowledge and skills to place material in whatever media will best serve the theater.

Often, a small theater has one person who combines the duties of audience development and public relations.

Richard Frankel was marketing director of New York City's Circle Repertory Company. In the fall of 1982, he was appointed managing director.

*   *   *

"I grew up in Brooklyn and was a stage manager for high school theater productions. I majored in television production in college and after graduation joined the Peace Corps. When I returned, I had no idea what to do. I was living in an apartment with some friends and one of them told me about a job as sound man at the Mercer Arts Center [a former New York City off-off-Broadway theater]. I went over there and got the job. From there I moved on to stage manager at Mercer and then at the Chelsea Theater Center. After a while, though, I wanted to do other things with my life. During production, stage managers work three to four weeks of fourteen-hour days. It was totally inconceivable for me to have a family or what I thought was a real life, so I decided that I wanted to get into management.

"Well, I couldn't get a job. I had gotten pigeonholed as a stage manager and no one would hire me as a manager. I got a job as box pusher and pipe carrier at the New York Shakespeare Festival and then got an office job at Queens College. I was making a lot of money but it wasn't for me. I wanted to be in the theater.

"I did have some luck because I was able to get a job at the Ensemble Studio Theatre [a nonprofit, New York City–based producing organization] as a general administrative person. It was terrific, because I had to do everything and wasn't expected to know a tremendous amount because I was being paid so little. I did fund raising, handled the theater's maintenance, made sure coffee was available during rehearsals, did cast contact sheets, selected pictures, and acted as press agent. I also got to know all the people at the foundations.

"From there, I got hired by the PAF Playhouse [Performing Arts Foundation Playhouse, a regional theater in Huntington, New York, which is now closed]. They had one large theater, a two-hundred-fifty-seat theater, four companies which presented children's plays, a touring program, and artist-in-residence programs. It was a real big job. All these productions needed programs, notices had to get in the papers, and on top of that, I was expected to get the New York press and critics to attend and review productions which were held in the large theater. (It is hard enough to get New York critics to attend off-Broadway productions located in New York. Getting them to Huntington, Long Island, is no easy task.) I offered a door-to-door service and drove them from New York out to PAF. It was a wonderful way to get to know the critics.

"Working at PAF showed me how the large regional theaters function. They are able to tap into their communities in a way that it is simply impossible to do in New York City. The local regional theater is a big deal in its community. The PAF board of directors had all these Long Island powerhouses on it and they could mobilize people for anything. Here at Circle Rep, we're just one out of so many others. While I was at PAF, I was offered the job at Circle Rep with the mandate to build the audience.

"My duties involve three things: press relations, institutional promotion, and marketing/sales. About forty percent is press relations; forty percent marketing/sales; and twenty percent institutional promotion.

"As press agent, I deal with the national and New York press on a per production basis. I do what any press agent does: oversee the show's program and try to get feature stories, television breaks, column items, and of course, critics. But I'm always looking to push the institution. We are not just selling individual plays. We are selling Circle Rep and its particularly unique sensibility and point of view. We hope that critics will see each work in the context of a body of work.

So we try to set a tone whereby it is obvious that Circle Rep is more than its individual productions.

"I also oversee annual reports and institutional brochures which describe Circle Rep and its events and programs. I write sections of funding proposals which are sent out to government agencies, corporations, and foundations.

"In terms of marketing and sales, we have found that the best way to sell tickets is through subscription campaigns, and the best way to sell subscriptions is by direct mail. That is my responsibility. I conceive subscription campaigns, write the brochures, supervise the design, and handle all the computer work involved in selecting lists of people to whom we will send the direct-mail pieces. Selling subscriptions is essential for our survival. When I first came here, I ran Circle Rep's first real subscription campaign. The first year, our subscribers went from seven hundred twenty to thirty-three hundred. The second year, we went to forty-two hundred and now, just over two years later, we are at five thousand eight hundred sixty-one.

"Direct mail is magic. We spend almost fifty thousand dollars doing it, but it will bring us almost three hundred fifty thousand. That's a lot of cash. You spend all this money on the campaign and send out all this material. Then there's a lull and you start having nightmares. But all of a sudden, the money starts coming in. We spend about eighteen dollars to get someone through the mail, but it's worth it. Subscribers renew fairly regularly and stay with us for an average of two-point-seven years. They also buy T-shirts and other merchandise, give special donations over and above the cost of their subscription, and buy extra tickets for special events.

"You have to understand how direct mail works if you are going to do it successfully. List selection and return analysis is now computerized. I go to seminars on marketing where I am the only arts person. Everyone else is selling widgets and industrial items. But compared to the arts, they're light years ahead of how we do things.

"Theater is probably the hardest arts field to work in. Fewer people are interested in it. It functions with less money than anything else. The hours are long. But I think that part of its great appeal is that it is all-consuming.

"Audience development! Does it exist in the music business? The movie business? What we deal with all the time is a real minority interest. Very, very few people anywhere are interested in theater, and especially Circle Rep's kind of theater. We can't compete with Rex Harrison in *My Fair Lady* and even Rex Harrison can't compete with the movies.

"But the great thing about working for an institutional theater like Circle Rep is that I get to do it all: marketing, press, and promotion. And I'm in the theater."

Commercial Theater

Press Agent

In the commercial theater, the producer hires a press agent to handle all press and publicity for a show. On Broadway, off-Broadway, national and touring companies, pre-Broadway tryouts, and bus-and-truck tours, the press agent must be a member of ATPAM. This is the same union to which company managers and house managers belong. There are approximately 200 press agent members of ATPAM.

Only five press agent apprentices are admitted to ATPAM each year. There is an apprentice program that consists of a series of seminars and the completion of an examination. An apprentice must accumulate a total of sixty weeks' credit during which time he apprentices to an ATPAM press agent who must be working, on contract, for a show. Forty of these

weeks can be accumulated the first year of the apprenticeship, but the remaining twenty cannot be obtained until the
third year. Although exceptions are made, the apprenticeship
must be completed within five years. As most shows do not
run very long, it can be difficult to accumulate the number of
necessary credit weeks unless you are apprenticed to one of
the few theatrical offices that handles the majority of shows.
Many more people hope to be press agents than can be accepted into ATPAM. Usually, apprentices have spent several
years in low-paying, often menial press assistant positions before being sponsored by an ATPAM press agent.

The press agent oversees all advertising. He is in charge of
obtaining all photographs and artwork that decorate the front
of the theater. The press agent announces the show to the
press, assumes the responsibility for press and critic coverage
on opening night, makes sure that photos and information are
sent to the appropriate media, and of course works hard to
get as much publicity for the production, its stars, and supporting personnel as possible. Press agents frequently plan
stunts. These are carefully planned events, which are designed to look spontaneous but which are really created by
the press agent in the hope that television news crews and
newspaper photographers will attend. The press agent hopes
to see the results on the evening news or in the next day's
newspapers.

Fred Nathan is a theatrical press agent whose shows have
included *The Little Foxes, Joseph and the Amazing Technicolor Dreamcoat, Sophisticated Ladies,* and *Cats.*

* * *

"When I was sixteen, I got a summer job as a messenger at
Blaine Thompson [a theatrical advertising agency]. I'd always
gone to the theater and I got the job because my cousin was

the art director. It was awful. The city was really hot and I was running around all day. I worked there for two summers in a row. But while I was there, I went to every theatrical office in the city and got to meet producers, press agents, and managers.

"After I graduated from high school, I went to Boston University. That first summer, I was able to get a job with a theatrical press agent in New York. I worked at her office for four months and then went back to Boston. I started going to every pre-Broadway tryout in Boston, which just made me ache for New York. I decided to quit school and come back. I got a job typing while trying to reestablish myself in a press office. After four months, I got a job with the late Saul Richmond.

"I had heard that he was a real character and I wanted to give him a reason to stop and pay attention to me. I went to Nathan's Famous and bought a hot dog and french fries. I put them in one of those plastic takeout boxes and attached a note saying: 'Nathan's are not only famous as Nathan's Famous for their hot dogs but also for their hot minds. Hire me.' And I got the job.

"Saul was a real hollerer, but a great teacher. I did everything in his office. I answered phones, sent out press releases, did billing, stuffed envelopes, handled critics, wrote releases, and handled tickets."

In addition to handling press and critic tickets for opening night, press agents receive a certain number of prime location seats for each performance. These are called press seats and are given out free to members of the working press or may be sold as house seats to those whom press agents want to extend the courtesy.

"I had gotten my union apprenticeship. My four months

working for the press agent during school had helped, as did my time at Blaine Thompson, and I was accepted the first time I went before the apprentice committee. But after fifteen months, I started getting restless. I was working on shows like *Let My People Come* and Jones Beach productions. I decided that I wanted to work in a bigger office where there were more prestigious shows . . . real Broadway shows.

"I started to send notes around and got a job at Solters and Roskin. [One of the biggest agencies in the business, they handle films and personalities including Barbra Streisand and Frank Sinatra, in addition to theatrical productions.] I started working on *Pippin* and *Same Time, Next Year*. I almost finished my apprenticeship there but quit to go work for someone else. I had found myself stuck doing 'go-fer' work and this other office agreed to put me on a show where I could handle the whole thing. It was *Do You Turn Somersaults?* which starred Mary Martin. It closed quickly and I then went back to Solters and Roskin, but this time in a very different way. I came back as a press agent and started working on the Ringling Brothers' Circus and *Hello Dolly*. Then I was assigned to work on *Stop the World, I Want to Get Off*, which was starring Sammy Davis, Jr.

"I was really scared every time I had to do a show by myself, which only made me work harder. I remember going to Chicago to see *Stop the World* before it came to New York. I got into a limo with the producer and his first question was, 'What are the numbers in New York?' I said, 'What do you mean?' Here I was supposed to be a press agent and I didn't know that 'numbers' meant advance sale.

"The show was a flop, but I had a great time working on it. After that, I had the opportunity to take *Hello Dolly* on the road. It was a relatively short tour: seven weeks in Washington, D.C.; one week in Orlando; two weeks in Miami; and five weeks in Baltimore. I got to know what it is like to handle a show on the road. You not only do a press agent's job but you also do marketing. You go to the box office and look at the wraps [the amount of money one show takes in]. Based upon that, you decide how much money should be spent on advertising. I was flying back and forth between cities, advancing the show and taking the star, Carol Channing, to interviews.

"When *Hello Dolly* closed, I took *Dracula* on the road. Solters and Roskin had handled both those shows, and although I did them as an independent contractor, my connection with the agency obviously made a difference in getting work. At that point I was thinking about how to get my own clients, and after a four-week period during which I was unemployed, I got a call from a general manager asking me if I would take *Oklahoma* on the road. I was very pleased to be called and decided to ask for two things: more than the union minimum wage and a commitment that if the show came into New York I would handle it.

"It was a great tour and I decided that once we got to San Francisco, I would not only handle that city but set up the rest of the tour from there. I kept in contact with the local promoters and sent out all the ads, releases, features, photos, and press kits. I also set up phone interviews for the cast in the various cities we were going to play."

A road or national company of a Broadway show has all the promotional material prepared in advance and sent to each city. Often, the press agent and advertising agency prepare flyers, ads, and window cards and just leave space for the local promoter to imprint the name of the theater, performance schedule, and ticket prices.

"The tour went to eight cities and lasted almost a year. By

the end of the Chicago engagement, we realized that *Oklahoma* would be coming to New York. I was thrilled, because it meant that I would have my own show on Broadway. I rented a room in another press agent's office and *Oklahoma* opened in December 1979.

"It was a great opening night. The stars of the original production were there and came up onstage after the show. The governor of Oklahoma attended and we had an actual surrey with a fringe on top outside the theater. We got a lot of press coverage. *Oklahoma* ended up running ten months, which gave me time to set up my own office."

Following *Oklahoma*, Nathan was hired to be press agent for the 1980 season's most eagerly anticipated musical, *42nd Street*. He was only twenty-five years old. *42nd Street* marked the return of producer David Merrick and director-choreographer Gower Champion to the theater. Both had left for Hollywood in order to work in film. Merrick, who had produced more than eighty-five shows on Broadway, had a reputation as one of the business's most flamboyant and demanding producers.

42nd Street first went to Washington, D.C., for its pre-Broadway tryout. When it came to New York, instead of beginning previews as most shows do, Merrick decided to go back into rehearsal. No opening date was set. This generated a lot of publicity, especially since there were rumors of disagreement between Merrick and Champion. Publicity increased when Merrick started running previews, but only allowed a limited number of people to attend. When Merrick refused to allow a *New York Times* writer who had been assigned to write a story about *42nd Street* to attend a preview performance, the show began to get daily press.

42nd Street finally opened in August 1980. It was a smash.

But after the cast had taken an unprecedented ten curtain calls, Merrick appeared on stage to announce Gower Champion's death. Champion had become fatally ill during *42nd Street*'s Washington engagement. Although he had continued working, he had entered a New York hospital a few days before *42nd Street* opened, and died the day of the opening.

"Monday night was opening. It was a fabulous opening. But during intermission, I came out into the theater and a reporter from the *Daily News* came over to me and said, 'Fred, what's this about Gower Champion being dead?' I knew that Gower had been sick after the first preview, but I didn't know how sick he was. He had taken some time off, but he worked like a dog. My last contact with him had been at the New York photo call where he set up all the photos and ran it.

"I went backstage to see Merrick and said, 'The press is on top of me. They say that Champion died.' And Merrick said, 'He did.'

"I quit *42nd Street* about six weeks after it opened. I had been fired and rehired, but it was all getting to be too much. At that point I was handling a revival of *Brigadoon* and I heard about *Sophisticated Ladies*, which was going into production. I went after that show. I called managers and everyone I thought might put in a good word for me. All five producers came to interview me and I got the show.

"The most important thing for me to do when I get a show is to make sure that it is announced properly. I want to go to *The New York Times*, *Daily News*, and *New York Post* and say, 'It's happening.' We may not have a theater; we may not have a date; and we may not have a star yet. With *Sophisticated Ladies*, we had stars and a theater and we pretty much knew our date. It was announced in the *Times*' theater col-

umn. [*The New York Times* publishes a weekly theater column. Press agents want to get their shows announced in that
column. Since *The New York Times* is the most important
publication for a show, it demands and receives an exclusive
on the announcement. This means that no announcement is
sent to other publications until *The New York Times* decides
whether or not to run it.] We followed that up with a press
release. This is a long release which tells every detail you
have to know about the show. After that, releases are only
sent out if it is necessary to correct something or give out new
information like the box office opening.

"Basically, my responsibilities are to get publicity and
oversee an advertising campaign. I also take care of critics on
opening night and seat them."

In the theater there are lists of critics and drama editors
and writers who are invited to opening night and what is
called second night, which is a performance either next or
close to opening night. Those who work for daily newspapers
and radio and television stations come to opening night. The
second-string critics, those who work for weekly publications
and are not on an overnight deadline, come to second night.
The press agent assigns seats to all these people. There is a
protocol to this seating. The press agent must know who sits
in front of whom, who sits on the aisle, and so forth.

"I get photos placed in publications and make sure that all
of the free listings in newspapers and magazines are done. I
also prepare the program which is distributed to the audience
for each performance and the souvenir book which is sold in
the lobby of the theater. The souvenir book is only done if the
show is a hit.

"A show like *Sophisticated Ladies* is an example of what a
show used to be like. We played four weeks in Philadelphia

and five weeks in Washington, D.C., before opening in New York. I set up a lot of publicity in Philadelphia and Washington, but we weren't selling tickets. In Washington we had over thirty interviews scheduled on radio and television and in the newspapers. There were a lot of problems with the show. We had good notices from *The Washington Post* and bad ones from *The Washington Star*.

"After the Washington opening, the producers decided to fire Gregory Hines, who was one of the stars [and got extraordinary reviews when the show finally opened in New York]. The company refused to go on without him and everyone ran to the airport and train station to find him. He was found, rehired, and went on that night. However, the same day, the director, stage manager, and assistant stage manager quit. A new director came in, but when I got back to New York I assumed the show would be a flop and was really depressed.

"We had set up a lot of preopening publicity in New York though. We.were able to get fashion layouts in *Vogue* and *Harper's Bazaar* for Judith Jamison [star of the Alvin Ailey American Dance Theater and making her theatrical debut]. We also invited people from every black-oriented radio station and pastors from black churches. We wanted to get word of mouth going about the show during its New York previews.

"I think that the most important thing for a show is word of mouth. Advertising can help sell tickets, with publicity reinforcing the advertising. But publicity can't sell a bad show. Hit shows also need publicity. It's important to maintain that feeling of being a hit show through constant visibility.

"When *Sophisticated Ladies* came into New York, the audiences started cheering after each preview. I couldn't believe it. It was the greatest feeling in the world. It ended up getting the best reviews of any show in the last five years, except maybe for *Annie*. We were a smash. And, of course, it was easy to get publicity for a show which received those kind of reviews.

"If a show opens with mixed reviews, it's very hard. When I handled *The First* [a musical about the great Brooklyn Dodger baseball player, Jackie Robinson], we got a tremendous amount of preopening publicity. There was television and magazine coverage . . . the kind of stuff you get when people really feel a show will be important. [However, when *The First* opened, it didn't get good reviews and closed after four weeks.] After opening, it was hard. You have to go to the press, who are lethargic about doing anything because critics really weren't up about the show. Sometimes you start calling your friends in the media for favors. It's horrible to have a show that just crawls along. It's much better to have a real hit or a real flop."

One of the things that a press agent does is create stunts. Stunts are carefully planned events to which the press is invited. The hope is that the stunt will generate media coverage.

"I do stunts, but I'm scared of them because they don't always work. I prefer to call them events. While I was working for Saul Richmond, he was handling *Moonchildren* off-Broadway. He sent out an announcement saying that John Glenn would be coming to the theater on the anniversary of his trip into space. Well, the place was full of press and in walked Saul, wearing a space outfit. It was outrageous, but it got a lot of press.

"For *Sophisticated Ladies*, we got New York City to proclaim the A train the 'Duke Ellington Express.' We had press cover that event from the platform of the Fifty-ninth Street subway station. When *Little Johnny Jones* opened with Donny Osmond, we had a high school band playing on Fifty-second Street.

"What is really important for a show, particularly a long run, are column items. [Those are the small news items that appear in nationally syndicated columns like Liz Smith and Earl Wilson.] They keep the name of the show alive, because there is no way you can get a feature story every day. I'm always on the lookout for items. I get them by looking at feature stories that have been done and pulling appropriate news items. Or I talk with actors in the company. You can often get items by reading *Variety* and seeing the show's weekly box office gross. Columnists like to report when a show is establishing records or doing very well.

"The other great outlet is when celebrities come to see the show. I ask them to go backstage and arrange for them to pose for a picture with the cast. You can often get a wire service break [Associated Press or United Press International, which service material to hundreds of newspapers throughout the country]. It's wonderful to think that someone was at the show on Thursday night and on Friday the picture appeared in a newspaper in Albuquerque."

Sometimes a press agent tries to avoid press coverage and publicity. This is particularly true when a superstar is involved.

"When I handled *The Little Foxes* with Elizabeth Taylor, we had the biggest star ever. She generates her own press and the job is significantly different. You have to try to keep press away. You try to keep things that are private secret, or things that are nobody's business quiet. It's very hard and it doesn't always work. I always waited for the press to call me about Liz. I never called them. I also don't lie to the press, ever. But I will say, 'That's something about Elizabeth's personal life that I will not talk about' or just 'No comment.'

"When she was sick before *The Little Foxes* opened, I had to answer a lot of questions. One of the positive things about dealing with such a celebrity is that you get the opportunity to deal with press other than the theater press. You get to know different people. That way, when you are handling something theatrical but which also involves news, you can call someone on the city desk and try to get it on the news pages rather than in back in the theater pages."

Although he is only in his late twenties, Nathan has had stunning success in only a few years.

"There's nothing extraordinary about what I do or what any other press agent does. You really end up getting certain shows because you have a relationship with the producer or your personality meshes well with another producer's. I don't feel secure about my business at all. I'm afraid it's going to fall apart every day.

"I also work very hard. It's very hard for me to make plans for myself in the evening. I can rarely take a vacation. I'm on call like a doctor. It's sometimes very hard for me to maintain my energy. But it's true that once you start getting shows, everything starts to roll and if a producer likes you, he stays with you."

Advertising

Advertising includes the advertisements taken in newspapers and magazines, commercials aired over radio and television, and posters displayed in windows, on billboards, and on busses and subways. Unlike publicity, which is free, advertising time and space are purchased.

Advertising has become increasingly important to the commercial theater. Whereas theatrical advertising used to be almost exclusively limited to print and occasionally radio, television is now utilized as an advertising vehicle. Currently, there are only two advertising agencies that handle the bulk of all Broadway and off-Broadway shows.

Theatrical advertising is different from what most people think of as "Madison Avenue." Advertising budgets, even for high-cost musicals, are significantly lower than for the smallest product. In addition, commercials and advertisements are frequently prepared and produced literally on a day's notice, which is something the larger Madison Avenue agencies are unaccustomed to. Unlike product advertising, market research and long-range planning aren't relevant to the theater. Rather, experience in the workings of the theater and the ability to take the essence of a particular theatrical offering and translate it to the public are the keys to theatrical advertising.

Jeff Ash is a founder and partner in Ash/LeDonne Inc., the agency that has handled *Nine, Sophisticated Ladies, Woman of the Year, Amadeus,* and many other Broadway and off-Broadway shows.

*   *   *

"My dad was in the business for many years. He was one of the owners of Blaine Thompson, which was the oldest advertising agency in the country. They always handled about seventy to eighty percent of all Broadway shows.

"When I graduated from college, I really wanted to produce, so I went to work for producer Stuart Ostrow, who was producing *The Apple Tree.* I worked as a general office assistant and helped out in the press office of Solters and Sabinson [later Solters and Roskin]. I started getting a good and varied background in the workings of the theater. When *The Apple Tree* closed, I went to work for some other producers, again as an assistant.

"Right about that time, I was asked to come and work at Blaine Thompson. My father had been ill and since I knew so many people in the business and had a general idea of how the advertising business operated, I was needed. So I went to work and started to learn about what is really involved in handling shows.

"I started by doing the ABCs which were, and still are, the backbone of what we do. [ABCs are small advertisements, all placed together, which appear in daily newspapers. They list, alphabetically by title, current Broadway and off-Broadway shows, their performance schedules, and ticket prices. These are paid advertisements and should not be confused with the free listings that magazines and newspapers often offer theatrical productions.] I also began to learn about advertising schedules, budgets, and, just how the business of theatrical advertising works in general.

"Just about that time, Peter LeDonne, my present partner and a friend of mine since college, joined Blaine Thompson as a copywriter. We had been trying to convince some of the producers that television was a viable means of advertising for the theater. Newspapers were and still are important, but we thought that television could bring in a whole new audience. It had never really been done before. Sometimes, there would be a simulated spot using some slides. Or occasionally, we would line up a well-known television personality and invite him to see the show on opening night. The next morning we would film him in front of the theater while he talked about the show and its reviews. We always bought the television time for the late news of the day following the opening.

The spot would run once and the idea was to try and get the whole thing to look like news. That was about the only television advertising the theater ever used.

"Together, Peter and I convinced Stuart Ostrow to do a television commercial for the musical *Pippin*, which had been running for six months and was beginning to feel a dent in its box office. We found a little studio in Princeton, New Jersey, and shot the commercial there in order to avoid some of the union costs. Ostrow had to take money away from print advertising in order to afford the ad. But a large new audience appeared, and *Pippin* ran at full capacity for the next two and a half years.

"Prior to the success of the *Pippin* ad, there had been two schools of thought about television advertising and the theater. One, people who watch television don't go to the theater, and two, the costs of making a television commercial are prohibitive. And it's true that when you make a television commercial, you do pay the unions. [Actors, musicians, stagehands all get extra fees and salaries.] But it was obviously worth it. Theater is a visual experience, and when we can take a piece of it and entice the audience to want to come and see more, we are being successful.

"My father died and Blaine Thompson was sold. Peter and I decided that the time had come for us to open up our own agency. There were a lot of things we didn't know about running an advertising agency so we decided to speak to some Madison Avenue agencies about becoming a subsidiary. We thought we could use their expertise in marketing, research, and time buying. None of those things had been used in theater before and we thought that perhaps they would be of benefit to us. We did find an agency that was anxious to have us and became their subsidiary for about a year and a half. Our offices remained here in the theater district and we maintained our own self-image. But we discovered that most of what we hoped to get from the agency we could do better ourselves.

"Madison Avenue agencies just are not geared towards the way theater operates. There is a lot of minutia in theater advertising which the larger agencies just can't or aren't inclined to do. They are used to dealing with products like Ford automobiles or packaged cereals, which have ongoing lives. They do research, product testing, and marketing studies. What we found was that by the time we got any advice or information, the show would have closed. There is an immediacy to theater advertising which just isn't true for anything else. For a national product, if the ad doesn't appear this week it's okay, because the week after the product will still be there. That's not true for theater.

"Also, the budgets are much larger on Madison Avenue. In the theater, you sometimes have twenty-five hundred dollars to buy radio time. And you must get that time, create the commercial, and put the ad on the air the next day. A Madison Avenue agency is used to a hundred-thousand-dollar budget for a radio ad. It is very difficult for them to concentrate on such a small budget. But in the theater, it's a lot of money and crucial for the show.

"The way we operate with our theater clients is that the producer contacts us. He brings us a script or sometimes just an outline. The account supervisors and I meet and decide who we think would be a good artist to do the artwork for the show. This artwork will be used for the poster and window cards and as a logo around which advertisements and front-of-the-house decoration are planned. We do about half a dozen pieces of art and present them to the producer and the show's creators.

"At the same time, we all get together to talk about the

various aspects of production. If the producer is taking the show out of town, we develop a print ad and often some radio commercials for the show to use in these out-of-town cities. We also start to work on the preopening schedule and advertising budget at that time. We plan announcement ads, a 'box office opens' ad, and a 'previews begin' ad."

The agency counsels the client about the size of the ads, the best time for them to appear, and the publications that should carry the ad. These are all budgetary considerations. Larger ads cost more, and some publications have higher advertising rates than others. One publication that is always used, however, is *The New York Times*. It is considered the most important publication for a theater ad and the most important review a production receives after opening.

"We also try to decide, at that time, whether a television commercial would be good for the show. If everyone decides to do one and the money is available, we try to shoot the commercial out of town, so that it is ready to air before the show opens."

The costs of a television commercial vary greatly. Depending upon the number of people used in the spot and how elaborate the commercial is, it can cost from twenty thousand to a hundred fifty thousand dollars. And in order for the commercial to be effective, a lot of money must be allocated to buy the time during which the commercial will be aired. These costs vary according to the season. Between Thanksgiving and Christmas, time is very expensive. But after New Year's, the cost plummets. Basically, though, it costs between fifteen and twenty-five thousand dollars a week to air a television commercial and all television commercials should be aired for a minimum of three to five weeks in order for the message to have an effect.

"We also decide how much to advertise before opening. If

there's really something to sell up front, we advertise more heavily. For instance, there might be a big star or, like in the case of *Evita*, there's a big word of mouth. In that case, we advertise heavily. However, if a show is coming in cold, the money is ill spent on lots of advertising. Most of the people at this agency have been involved in theater for a number of years and our decisions are based on a combination of accumulated knowledge and instincts.

"We often get involved in producing decisions. We will say whether a song works or offer advice about casting. We will say whether we think the show should go out of town or not. A producer may do anywhere from one to three shows a year. But we usually have fifty shows open in a season. So we have a lot of experience in what works and what doesn't work. We have a sense of why one theater might be better than another and even about the climate of the season. Sometimes it's better to wait before presenting the show.

"However, everything leads up to opening night. The critics are crucial. Immediately after the final curtain, we all go to the agency. We obtain all the newspaper reviews and listen to the television reviews. If the show doesn't do well, it often closes the same night. If it runs, we do layouts for quote ads in which the most positive lines from a review are taken and printed along with the reviewer's name. We have to decide what kind of ads to run. Do we run large half-page quote ads? Do we start a radio campaign? Should we add quotes to a preexisting television ad or leave it as it is? Sometimes the producer decides to do a television commercial after the reviews are in. An entirely separate campaign might be started. We often work all night after an opening.

"The most important thing to remember is that in order to sell a show, we need a good show. The thing that saves most shows is word of mouth. We can't save a show that is terrible and we probably don't make that much difference with a terrific show, although we can take credit for bringing it to the public's attention. A large number of shows, though, fall in between. In those cases, advertising makes a difference.

"For our theatrical agency to be successful, we must handle a hefty part of the business in order to offset the costs of those shows that simply open and close. We barely even cover our expenses before opening night. All the creative work must be done before opening even though little actual advertising gets placed. It's the long-running productions that support us.

"Basically, though, we have a good reputation and handle many of the big shows. But we have had to expand into other areas of entertainment and leisure-time activities. We feel that is what we know best and we are trying to grow into areas like hotels, movies, and outdoor theme parks. We have to, because although theater is our backbone and what we love, there just isn't enough of it to be our sole support."

Giving Life to the Show— The Creative Team

Casting

In order to fill the available roles in a production, most producers retain casting agents. In the commercial theater independent casting agents are hired for each show. Unlike agents who represent actors directly and receive a percentage or commission from those for whom they obtain work, casting agents are paid a fee and royalty by the production company. In regional and institutional theater, many of the larger organizations maintain their own casting departments.

Actors' Equity, the union for all performers in the legitimate theater, has a membership of about 28,000. With a regular unemployment rate of almost 80 percent, the competition for jobs among Equity members is fierce. Simply being seen by those in a position to offer employment is a difficult task for most actors. Casting agents are inundated by telephoned requests for interviews, photos, and résumés mailed by aspiring actors, and invitations to attend the numerous showcase productions held throughout New York

City where actors hoping to be seen by casting agents usually perform for no pay.

Casting agents do not actually hire actors. Rather, they are matchmakers, bringing actors and the production's creators together. Ultimately, it is the director, in collaboration with playwright and producer, who hires those to fill the available roles.

Julie Hughes and *Barry Moss* are partners in one of the busiest of the handful of casting agencies that work in the commercial theater.

* * *

"Back in the days when producers maintained their own offices, they had their own staffs of people who did casting. In the old days, producers knew who they wanted. They often selected plays with specific actors in mind. That generally isn't done much anymore. Today, there are many producers who produce only one show at a time, often waiting years between shows. They don't maintain offices and it is much cheaper in the long run to get a pick-up staff to work on each show.

"We get involved in the very beginning of the show. The producer or director comes to us with an idea. Sometimes there's not even a completed script, although we are finding that recently there is not so much lead time on a show. It's usually about six weeks. The theater becomes available, money comes in, and a star is ready. It all happens much faster now.

"We are hired to cast the show and retained to maintain the show for its entire run. We cast the national tour and all other companies. We are not hired to do chorus, although we will help if necessary. For instance, if the production is looking for a character soprano or short tenor, we go through our files. Basically, we are hired to fill the principal roles.

"We handle the entire audition. We book the space and hire readers. Sometimes during auditions the stage manager does the readings with potential actors, but we prefer to hire actors to read. We want to make sure that the person auditioning has someone to whom he can respond. The main purpose of what we are doing is to present the actor to the director in the best possible way. Actors often don't realize that, to some degree, we are as much on the line as they are. We are only as good as the actors we bring in. Actors often come to audition and think they are facing the enemy. We try to create an atmosphere in which actors can audition. We relax them, joke with them, and try to guide them. We know what the director is looking for and we advise actors about what they should wear, or if it's a musical, what they should sing. Basically, we really want the actor to get the job. If the first five actors who walk in are terrific and are hired, we've done a great job.

"As soon as we get the script, we start to talk over characters. We do a breakdown which goes to all the agents on the east and west coasts. [The breakdown is a list of all the available parts in a production, with a description of the characters and all criteria necessary to fill these parts, including physical type, age, vocal range, and appearance.] There is a new 'Breakdown Service' that mails the breakdowns to everyone in the business, and this saves us a tremendous amount of time. We also telephone actors' agents and explain the kind of project we are working on and tell them what we are looking for.

"Both of us work together on each project. There are times when one of us is out of the office or out of town. We must both know what's going on. We complement one another and our strong and weak points balance. We need to talk characters together and discuss the shows. We have two assistants and they are indispensable. There is an enormous amount of drudge work in casting which people don't understand. There are incredible amounts of phone calling in setting up auditions and a lot of paperwork.

"We keep alphabetical files on all people with whom we've ever worked or those whose work we've seen and liked. We keep notebooks on every show, which include all the audition and submission notes. That way, we can consult our notes and pick up people to whom we've responded in the past for other productions."

Agents represent actors and help them get work in return for a fixed percentage of the actors' earnings from any jobs obtained through the agent. The percentage is usually ten percent. When they receive copies of the breakdown, agents submit their clients' photos and résumés. Those who work with known theatrical names call the casting directors directly, working on a more personal basis. A casting director preparing a new show usually receives hundreds of photos and résumés from hopeful actors and agents.

One of the chronic laments among actors is the difficulty they have in getting auditions. All actors want to be seen by casting agents, because they are the link between those who hire—the director, playwright, and producer—and the actor. And casting agents do tend to be careful about the actors they submit for parts.

"If we trust an agent, we will screen a new submission of his. We are careful about bringing people to auditions whom we don't know. If we don't have rapport with an agent or know that we can't trust his judgment, we just don't do it. In essence what we are doing when we bring a person into an audition is putting our stamp of approval on that actor. We are saying that we approve of this person. There are some directors who will not be upset if someone isn't right for the role. But some directors will hit the roof and say, 'Don't you understand this show?'

"A lot of agents aren't doing what they should be doing. One of the things we notice is that agents never come with their clients to auditions anymore. When we first started, they used to. Now, they don't even come with major stars. They've also stopped calling and asking for feedback on their clients. We're certainly prepared to give them a response and tell them why their client didn't get the job. If we call an agent and ask for someone and the agent tells us that he is unavailable, the agent rarely suggests an alternative. It's like pulling teeth to get agents to submit their clients."

Actors' Equity requires all shows to hold Equity Principal Interviews (EPIs). These brief interviews are announced in the theatrical trade publications—*Backstage*, *Variety*, and *Show Business*—and give Equity members the opportunity to speak with a casting person and present photos and résumés.

"It's very hard to tell anything about people through interviewing. It only tells you what they look like. We much prefer to audition. We want to see someone read or sing. That's why EPIs are useless as far as we're concerned. We would like to change them into Equity Principal Auditions, where actors could do anything they wanted for five minutes. They could read, sing, whatever.

"We end up seeing as many as two thousand actors or as few as twenty. It depends upon the show and our relationship with the director. There are some directors with whom we've worked time and time again and we tend to know what they want. When the director doesn't know what he's looking for, it can be very frustrating. Sometimes it will take us a week to cast a show and sometimes it can take us eighteen months. The longest it ever took for us to cast a show was for one which opened and closed the same night.

"We find more and more, because of the theater's economics, that producers are looking for stars. Quite often a show has a run because it has a recognizable name. That same show without the star wouldn't have a chance. We can't always get the stars producers want. When it comes to stars, it works several ways. Sometimes a star is looking for a play. Sometimes a play has been developed around a star. That's a star vehicle and the star is part of the show. However, usually we lay the groundwork for the production. We approach the star's manager and check the star's availability and interest in doing theater. Then, if all the answers are affirmative, the director and producer often fly to California [where most stars with big box office appeal live] to speak with the star. A big star must be approached on a personal level.

"Basically our job, our gift really, is to tune into the way the director thinks. It might not be the way we think, but we must implicitly feel what the director wants for the show. We know our talent but we must have that instinct for what the director wants. We might cast one person for one director and never think of casting the same person for another director. We must respond to the director. His life is on the line to some degree when he's doing a show, and he has the final say in all casting decisions. We care and get terribly involved. There have been times when we've been deeply depressed at the end of a casting session and think that the wrong people have been cast. But the bottom line is that it is not our choice."

Just knowing possible talent is a full-time job. Casting agents are always on the lookout for new talent.

"We should watch every television show. There are all the

PBS shows filmed in New York, showcases off-off Broadway, and of course, all the shows on and off Broadway. We see every film which is shot in New York. We get numerous requests to see people's work. Between the four of us, we attend some event every single night. Each of us is out three to four nights a week doing something which is business related. Weekends, we often just watch television shows we have taped."

Hughes and Moss don't just cast for the theater. Increasingly, they work on television and film projects.

"We could not maintain an office of our own on our fees from the theater. And we are the most prolific casting office in the theater. If we do one film, we earn what we would get from four or five plays. In theater we make our money on long runs. We charge a fee for the casting and then a weekly fee or percentage during the show's run. It's not a lot each week, but if we have three or four shows running it comes to a fair sum. But being able to go back and see a wonderful performance and hear the audience respond to that performance is very gratifying. In the theater, there is an immediacy which nothing else has."

Directing

The director is responsible for the entire play. He takes the playwright's work and transforms it into a stage production, interpreting it through staging and character development. The director collaborates with the set, costume, lighting, and sound designers in order to present an integrated production that reflects his vision of the author's words.

The entire process of production revolves around the director. He makes the final casting decisions and practically always has approval of the designers chosen to work on the production. The director sets the tone for rehearsal and is responsible for its organization and timetable. Some directors allow actors great latitude in character development and interpretation, whereas others are adamant in expecting actors to adhere to a set interpretation of the work. Regardless, actors and often even the playwright are responsible to the director and it is he who bears responsibility for the final production.

Directors are represented by the Society of Stage Directors and Choreographers (SSDC), which is an independent national labor union.

Tony Tanner directed the Broadway production of *Joseph and the Amazing Technicolor Dreamcoat* and the revival of *A Taste of Honey*, which moved to Broadway after a not-for-profit, off-Broadway run. Other New York directorial credits include *Something's Afoot, Class Enemy*, and *Gorey Stories*.

* * *

"I started directing when I was in my late twenties. I was an actor and had planned to be a star. I was born in England and attended drama school there. When I graduated, I spent about five years in English repertory, performing in about two hundred fifty plays. I also stage-managed and now find that experience to have been immensely useful. It gave me the means to discover how all sorts of things can be done, which is important to know as a director. I also dressed sets— gathering books, pictures, and ornaments. That also turned out to be tremendously useful. My eye was constantly being developed.

"I got to London when a musical which I had written was optioned by Michael Codron, a producer/manager. In London I performed in several reviews for which I had written sketches. A small regional theater suggested that I write an entire review instead of single sketches. When it was completed, the producer and I sat down to discuss who should direct the show. Everytime he suggested someone, I made a face. Finally, he suggested that I direct it myself. It was called *New Brooms*.

"At that point, the only thing I felt confident about was my ability to get the best out of the material because I knew exactly how it should go. I was completely at sea about what the stage should look like or how it should be organized. I realized how much I had to learn and how many shortcomings I had.

"But things started to happen. I was asked to return to my drama school and direct some shows there. Then the Oxford Playhouse, one of Britain's regional theaters, asked me to direct Noel Coward's *Hay Fever*. I took it on because it was a tremendous challenge and I had been depressed by what I had done with my own play. I ended up doing three plays at Oxford and found myself hooked. I began to feel a lot better about myself as a director. But all this time, I was still planning to be a star.

"I came to the United States to take over Tommy Steele's role on Broadway in *Half a Sixpence*. I just fell in love with New York and applied for my green card [to receive permanent status as a resident of the United States]. I felt very much more at home in the United States than in England. It was very odd to feel, at the age of thirty-three, that I had been born in a foreign land and belonged somewhere else.

"I did a lot of work in the United States. I was with the Washington Shakespeare Festival as a director and actor. I acted in and directed *What the Butler Saw* at the Academy Festival Theatre and worked at Buffalo's Studio Arena Theatre. I directed a performance of *The Fantasticks* at Long Island's PAF Playhouse and joined a bus-and-truck tour of

George M. Then two events happened which made me consciously decide to become a director.

"I felt that my career was in a shambles. I had come to America as a star. After *Half a Sixpence* closed, I couldn't get any other work on that same level. I also formed a close relationship which continues today. I decided that if I wanted the emotional stability and security of the relationship, I would have to find a way of controlling my geographic whereabouts. You know, actors are bondsmen. They go on the road for months at a time and often have to travel in order to work. I remember calling Zoe Caldwell and asking her if she would come to Buffalo to play Queen Elizabeth in *Elizabeth the Queen*. She has a family and said, 'No dear. I've just directed my first play and realize that as a director you leave after the second day.' I knew that if I directed, even if I had to go out of town in order to do it, I could come back. So I decided to develop the directing part of my career. And in the last ten years, directing has taken over almost completely."

Two of the shows that Tanner directed in 1981, revivals of *A Taste of Honey* and *Joseph and the Amazing Technicolor Dreamcoat*, moved to Broadway after receiving critical acclaim off-Broadway.

Tanner had met *Joseph*'s creators, Andrew Lloyd Webber and Tim Rice, before coming to the United States. Residents of Great Britain, Webber and Rice had only recently formed their collaboration and were working on an oratorio based on a Bible story that evolved into *Joseph*. It was their first work. The team turned out to be very successful, creating *Jesus Christ Superstar* and *Evita*. However, *Joseph* was known primarily as a children's piece. Although it was produced a number of times, it never received very good reviews.

About five years ago, Tanner was asked to stage a production of *Joseph* for Los Angeles. Midway, however, the producer lost the rights and the project was canceled. However, Tanner always felt that *Joseph* could be staged successfully for an adult audience. When a New York production was planned, Tanner was asked to direct it.

Joseph was to open at the Entermedia Theatre, an off-Broadway house located on Manhattan's Lower East Side. The Entermedia has stage dimensions comparable to many Broadway theaters. Shows have been presented at the Entermedia with the hope that they would receive favorable reviews and then move to Broadway. Since sets are both the most expensive and time-consuming element of production, a show that moves from the Entermedia to Broadway can do so quickly and without the significant added expense of a new set. *Grease*, Broadway's longest-running musical, moved to the Royale Theatre from the Entermedia. *Joseph* did the same.

Directors usually start work on a show weeks, and often months, before rehearsals begin. If the production is a new work, the director and playwright collaborate. It has been said that the playwright is the architect and the director the builder. The director interprets the playwright's work and presents it to an audience. It is crucial that playwright and director not only share a similar vision but have a common understanding of the work to be presented. They must both see the same play.

"The only way I feel I can work with the playwright on revisions and make his play better is if I know that I understand the work in such a way that I can make it better in the way the playwright wants it to be better. That's the art of working with the playwright."

One of the reasons that new dramatic plays that appear on Broadway almost inevitably appear first in regional theater is that the not-for-profit sector is able to provide an environment where playwright and director can collaborate. The not-for-profit theater can offer space in which to work, staged readings, workshop performances, and, most of all, time in which to work on a play's development. But even if the work is not receiving a first production, it is the director who presents his personal vision of the play to the audience.

"It often takes several readings for me to get to the heart of a show. I have to close my eyes and see pictures of the stage. With *Joseph*, though, it was immediately available to me. Sometimes you read a script that you just feel will work. And when that happens, it's magic.

"With *Joseph*, I loved the *carte blanche* feeling about the show. I knew it had been done many times before, but I also knew it was wide-open territory. When people come to me with shows that already have lots of stage directions in the script and indications of how the scenery should look, I feel that half the joy is taken away. I love to do shows where I can be totally creative.

"I had a concept for *Joseph* which would have worked for Los Angeles. But when I saw the Entermedia, I knew that my Los Angeles idea wouldn't work. I realized that my original idea of having a unit set [one basic set which can be changed or adapted for different scenes] with people on platforms wouldn't work. I also decided that we should have girls instead of choirboys. I felt that the sexual tension created by having boys and girls on stage was important. From the start we had to establish the brothers' grievances with their brother Joseph. I wanted the audience to sympathize, or at least understand, why the brothers decide to get rid of Joseph. So right away, in the first number, I had all the girls go for Joseph.

"*Joseph* had always been presented as a spontaneous, almost knockabout work. This production is very formal and presentational. Each part comes right out to the audience. As a matter of fact, the producers' idea for the show was based upon the production that had been done at Ford's Theatre in Washington, D.C. They were frightened when they saw my first run-through, because my *Joseph* had a very strongly marked style. I wasn't prepared for the producers' shock when they first saw the show. Things were very tense for a while."

Since the blocking—the actual movements and actions performed by the actors on stage—are to a great extent determined by the stage's design and organization, the director works with the set designer from the very beginning of production. The director almost always has contractual approval of the designers, who execute the visual elements of the overall conception. Much of the production's development in its beginning stages must be based on an implicit and mutual understanding of the director's intentions.

"Usually the first thing I do after deciding to do a show is to meet with the designers. I go to the set and costume designer and say, 'This is the concept. This is how we will be working.' And, one of the things that happens in a show where so many people are involved is that they can stray from the agreed-upon concept. The wonder and terror of the musical theater is that you have to collaborate. You connect with other people, share ideas, and must be mutually creative. It's a wonderful sense of artistic communion, but it is a disaster if it doesn't work.

"When I meet the set designer, I show sketches I have made and discuss them in very pragmatic terms. I'm specific about the angle of an incline or how many feet high a certain level must be. I even specify the size of the treads on the stairs. Often, certain sizes work better for certain actions and it all comes down to what the actors can and must do.

"For *Joseph* I came up with the idea of three pyramids, all of which were to move. The designer suggested that the middle one be stationary and appear vast and almost endless in height. This is the kind of collaborative scheme that makes a work truly effective. But as much as you know and as many times as you've done it, there's still this tremendous anxiety about whether the concept will work physically as well as you hope it will. Ideally, you should be able to rehearse on the set. But usually you only get the cast on the set during previews and you end up adapting with opening night getting closer and closer every moment.

"While I am working with the designers, I am involved in preproduction, especially when I'm doing a musical. With *Joseph*, I spent about four days in a studio with my dance assistant and another dancer. We just blocked out the show. [This initial blocking is important for the purposes of set design, but it is also part of the director's preparation for rehearsal.] Since I know what the actors will have to negotiate on stage, it means that when I come into rehearsal, I'm ready to start staging right away. I always have a plan, but I'm also prepared to throw it all away if something better comes up. That's why it's so important to get the show up on its feet as soon as possible. I see something and I realize that it's not what I'd imagined at all. Each change leads to another change.

"I had *Joseph* staged within a week. I think it's important, because you must get the immediacy of your first reaction to the piece out on the stage as soon as possible. The theater is such a pragmatic business, and yet you must be able to conceptualize. I believe that the imaginative faculties are as important to a director as they are to an actor or writer. That first bit of staging is comparable to a first draft. Then I can look at it and go back for a second draft. After that, I can go back for a third draft and clean up bits and pieces that don't satisfy me."

Casting is among the most important responsibilities of the director. The director consults with the casting director, discussing concept and character. The casting director then screens possible actors and auditions them before the director. The final decision is the director's.

"I think that every director would agree that casting constitutes a very large part of what a director does. When you cast, you are absolutely committing yourself to a result. The work will stand or fall on the capabilities and suitability of the actors. Casting *Joseph* was hard. I don't think we completed the casting until four days before the first day of rehearsal.

"During casting, the concept undergoes changes as well. We decided to use a woman rather than a man as narrator rather late in the casting process. None of the men we saw seemed to have the quality for which we were searching. And we saw a tremendous number of boys, because I felt that they, the brothers, constituted the body of the show. When it came time to narrow it down from the final twenty or so, it was heartbreaking. You know, one of the nicest things in the theater is being able to give people jobs. But we wanted to find boys for whom we could create a particular and individual place in the show. As a matter of fact, when I was casting for the national company, I wanted to avoid duplicating the Broadway company. One of the charms of this production is that everybody has a moment which is created just for him."

Finally, of course, rehearsals begin. In the commercial theater, directors usually have four weeks of rehearsal time for a straight play and six for a musical. Then there are a series of previews during which the play is performed in front of an audience and changes made almost daily. Shows used to go out of town before opening in New York, but today few do because they simply cannot afford the costs. *Joseph* rehearsed in New York and then played about two weeks of previews before opening.

"On the first day of rehearsal, there is a meeting with everyone. The entire music staff, the cast, designers, producers, and press people are all there. Everybody is introduced and they see a model of the set and costume sketches. I give a little speech, the Equity representative takes care of business, and then we get down to work. For *Joseph* the first thing we did was learn the music. It is usually taught by the musical director, but I have something to say about everything—the tempo, phrasing, interpretation, and certainly diction.

"As a director, if I do anything consciously, it is to create a climate in which everyone feels secure. I'll never forget reading the foreword to Tennessee Williams's *Cat on a Hot Tin Roof*. When asked what director Elia Kazan's method of directing was, Williams had responded, 'Love.' Now I know that the word sounds like a terribly sentimental platitude, but it isn't at all. Williams means exactly what he says, and he must have searched hard before he used the word. When he came out with it, it was the truth. Kazan creates a climate in which people are totally secure. If you are secure, you can be courageous. You venture, you risk, you experiment, and you can come forth.

"I can't imagine how people direct without having acted. I don't think it matters if you are good or not as an actor, but in order to direct you must know how naked an actor feels. As a director, you have to get the actor to put out, to try. You say, 'Come on. Let's see what you can do with this.' And I think that actors can only do that when they feel secure, loved, approved, and accepted. I have to keep saying, 'Of course you can do that. That's why I asked you to and that's why you got the part.'

"There's always a proper balance in rehearsal. There are a lot of jokes but not too many. There must be a feeling that work is being done, but the tension must occasionally be broken. Obviously, I like people to like me and the 'love technique' could perhaps be called self-serving. But I also know that it's the best way to get results. I don't like making people afraid and I don't like alienating people. Of course, I do get angry sometimes, but most of the time it comes from frustration when I'm trying to get something that just won't come.

"I tend to be a quick person. My tempo is quick, I think quickly and I talk quickly. I also react quickly. But being a director means that I can't always be as fast as I want to be. For instance, when I was directing *Taste of Honey*, one of the actresses took a long time. I just had to wait. I knew that the performance would come and that when it did, it would be great. You just have to believe that it will come, because unless you've worked with someone before, you have no way of really knowing whether or not it will. You just hope and pray and must trust the instinct that made you cast that person. But the point is that everybody has their own tempo and you must be sensitive to that."

When a production moves into the theater, it is often just a few days before the first public performance. The cast is working ten-out-of-twelve-hour days, often in costume and makeup and under lights. The production starts its tech rehearsal, which marks the fusion of the acting and technical elements. This is often the point at which the director sees whether his vision has worked or not. Although changes, often major ones, are made during previews, those first days at the theater, where all the creative elements are brought together, can offer the final test of a director's conceptualization. *Joseph* had four days of tech and dress rehearsal before beginning its two weeks of previews.

"I got excited as soon as I walked into the theater. I saw that it was going to work. It was one of those rare events where it exceeded my expectations. It was even better than I thought it was going to be, which hardly ever happens. The show just bubbled."

After the opening, a show technically becomes the stage manager's responsibility. The stage manager becomes the director's representative at the theater, and, ideally, maintains the show so that it reflects the director's work, both concretely and conceptually. However, this postopening period is often problematic both for the director and the cast. Just as the playwright has to entrust his work to the director, the director must entrust his work to the actors who, in turn, must now carry the performance responsibility themselves.

"There is a period after opening when I don't know how to comport myself. I feel a terrible sense of loss. There have been these tremendously close relationships with the creative staff and the actors, and then the show opens. I sometimes feel like a specter at the feast because it's the actors' show after opening and they must take full responsibility for their performance at some point. I make myself let go but I also think I often underestimate the actors' sense of loss when I go away."

Although some directors really do leave, severing bonds completely and not even returning to direct new cast members or national companies, Tanner does return periodically to rehearse the company. He also casts and directs national companies.

"The cast finds it comforting when they know that I'm still involved. I also go back for my own reputation. If I've been praised for the show, I want to go on earning it. Yet there's a fine line between keeping the show fresh and harassing the company. It's basically their show after opening and that is the way it must be."

Stage Manager

Every show has a stage manager. The position ranges from working in a small community theater where the stage manager doubles as light and sound operator, performing other technical jobs as well, to large Broadway musicals where the stage manager oversees a staff of assistants and directs the operation of millions of dollars worth of equipment.

The job has come a long way from the time when the stage manager, who was often a former actor, stood in the wings with a promptbook, whispered missed lines to actors, and signaled the time for the curtain to drop. The growth of professional theater companies and technological innovations have created a need for skilled stage managers and made the position a real profession. Today, more often than not stage managers receive billing on all production material along with the other creative staff.

The actual number of stage managers working on a show depends upon its size. A drama with one set probably requires only a single stage manager and an assistant who might play a small role in the show as well. Larger shows have several stage managers who fall into one of several categories.

The *production stage manager* (PSM) is in charge of everything that happens in the backstage area (technically everything that happens from the proscenium arch back). He must have technical skills and understanding, as he is responsible for making sure that all production elements (lights, sets, costumes, sound equipment) are completed and functional in time for opening night. The production stage manager is an organizer and facilitator. He coordinates rehearsal schedules, costume fittings, preopening press activities, and every other piece of business that concerns the company of actors and creative people. He must be a diplomat, able to deal with people. He works with a company of actors and creators who inevitably are tense, exhausted, and worried before opening. And since the production stage manager is the only person who has contact with each individual connected with the show, he tends to be the recipient of everyone's anxieties and problems and is often called upon to soothe and support.

The production stage manager must work well with the director. After opening, he maintains the show. He conducts understudy rehearsals and deals with actors and their problems, personal or professional. He puts new cast members into the show and must be constantly vigilant in making sure that the performances remain alive and fresh. Sometimes, production stage managers direct national or road companies when the director is unavailable.

The *stage manager* usually runs the show. During the performance, he stands at an offstage desk in the wings and "calls the show" from a promptbook, which is a copy of the script in which every cue for light, sound, or scene change is recorded. The stage manager transmits these cues to the technicians, who actually handle the equipment and effect the change.

Often, the stage manager cannot see the technicians and stagehands who receive the cues. There are connecting systems of lights that go on and off, indicating cues. The stage manager wears a headset through which he can transmit cues verbally. The stage manager may have a closed-circuit television monitor mounted above the desk from which he can see various parts of the theater, including the parts of the stage that are not visible from his vantage point.

Assistant stage managers (ASMs) do all the things that the production stage manager and stage manager are too busy to do. They help call the show and assist with the numerous details involved in opening and maintaining a show. These can range from taking phone messages, compiling cast contact sheets, and sweeping the floors during rehearsal to checking and making sure that complicated stage equipment is in working order before each performance.

Stage managers are members of Actors' Equity. There are some situations in which stage managers do not have to be union members, but if they are working with an Equity company of actors or in a theater that has an Equity agreement, they must join the union.

Peter Lawrence is a production stage manager whose Broadway credits include *The First, Annie, The Suicide,* and *An Almost Perfect Person.*

* * *

"I was going to be a lawyer and went to college to study political science. In the middle of my freshman year, however, I was so bored that I decided I simply had to do something else. I called home and told my mother, who said, 'Well, what do you like to do?' I said, 'I like the theater.' So she suggested I take some theater courses. And that's what I did.

"I ended up at Ohio State, where I had been offered a scholarship, and majored in directing. After graduation, I was offered a job as technical director at Transylvania College in Lexington, Kentucky. The college had opened a brand new two-million-dollar arts center. For a hundred dollars a week, I managed it. I was in charge of the entire physical plant and also taught various theater courses. When the administration decided to use the space for presenting outside shows, I was given eleven thousand dollars to book shows. I flew to New York, met with Tom Mallow of American Theatre Productions, and began booking bus-and-truck productions into the theater. It was my first taste of producing.

"After two years, I decided to go to graduate school. I decided upon the University of Hawaii because I liked their program and because they taught Japanese and Chinese theater. I sold everything and went to Hawaii.

"I eventually founded my own theater, the Hawaii Performing Arts Center, which still exists today. I directed and wrote plays. We toured all around the islands. I got further and further away from the university and eventually dropped out of the master's program. My life was wonderful. But one day I just decided that I had to move on. Hawaii was just too good. It was a place to end up, not a place to start out. So I decided to move to New York.

"I didn't know anyone in New York except three slight acquaintances. I called one of them when I arrived and he suggested I call the Mercer Arts Center as they were looking for someone to sell tickets. I was looking for a survival job, I didn't want to act but figured I would direct and write. So I took a job as day treasurer while I thought about what I wanted to do. I decided to get into management and worked for a while in management at Mercer Arts Center. I realized that I was not only terrible at management but also hated it. For a while I tried taking pictures for résumés. But basically, I was doing nothing and had to borrow money to get by.

"One day, I got a call from someone who had been a stage manager at the Mercer Arts Center. He had become the executive producer for a chain of dinner theaters, Country Dinner Playhouses. They were doing *The Ninety Day Mistress* in Austin, Texas, and he asked me to work with the director, who was rehearsing the company in New York. He wanted me to be stage manager and, of course, when asked, I said I had had stage-managing experience.

"The director and I worked very well together and I seemed to have an aptitude for stage management. I was asked to go to Texas to stage-manage the show there, and following that I was asked to stage-manage *Born Yesterday* starring Janis Paige for Country Dinner Playhouse in Florida. I said yes but insisted it be an Equity job so I could get into the union. I ended up being stage manager for all their productions. There were some proscenium stages and some arena stages and I had to restage all the shows from arena to proscenium. I replaced actors, did casting, and was technically responsible for the shows. It was wonderful. We did a new show every four weeks. There would be an eight-day rehearsal period, the show would open, and I would spend the next two weeks flying from theater to theater.

"From there things proceeded logically. I worked in stock and was asked to come back to New York to do some off-Broadway work. My real break came when I was working at Chicago's Arlington Park Theatre. Colleen Dewhurst was starring in a new play, *An Almost Perfect Person*, which was being directed by Zoe Caldwell. The show wasn't successful, but a New York producer picked up the option and we tried out the show throughout the country on tour. We made a lot of changes, and midway through this summer tour Zoe had to leave in order to film *The Seagull* for the BBC. So I was left in charge of the show. Zoe came back, more work was done, and eventually we opened at the Belasco Theatre in New York. That was in 1977. It had taken me five years from the time I arrived in New York to get to Broadway.

"After that, I did only one more off-Broadway show. I had gotten discouraged about stage managing after working off-Broadway a lot of the time. Off-Broadway you run the lights, do the sound . . . just about everything. It's a great training ground and gives you your legs, but I thought that I didn't want to work that way all the time. So I went on the road and worked on several national companies, including *Timbuktu* and *Annie*, which I did for about nine months. Now I'm able to work in New York most of the time. But the only way I got off the road was just refusing to go. I simply had to say that I couldn't go anymore."

Production stage managers start work during preproduction, before rehearsals begin. They used to be in charge of auditions, but today most productions retain outside casting directors. However, if there is no one else in charge of casting, the stage manager runs the auditions. He keeps track of all performers seen and notes the director's comments about each actor on cards that are filed and retained. These records are vital. If a director decides that he wants to see a certain actor again, the stage manager must know how to reach that actor. In addition, the notes are important when a replacement is sought or casting is being done for national or touring companies.

"I run the auditions except if there are casting people. But I am there. I bring people in and out and sometimes do readings with auditioning actors. Sometimes I make the deal on the rehearsal space, although that is usually the general manager's job.

"Then I meet with each designer. I have to find out how much time it is going to take to accomplish everything. I must know how long it will take to make the set and how much time the load in will take. I am concerned with backstage spacing. I must know how much storage space there is offstage, where the spotlight positions will be, and from which position the show will be called. You can have a real nightmare if you don't handle these things well in advance. I have even forced set designers to do storage plots which show exactly and to scale where each unit will be placed offstage. Sometimes, the set must be redesigned because it just cannot be stored in the theater as originally planned. I also make sure we have prop tables backstage and quick-change booths when necessary. And I want to know exactly where they will be situated.

"Before we start rehearsals, I work out schedules. I decide how much time we will need to tech the show and how much time we will need for dress rehearsal. I try to make sure that the director will have the time he needs with the cast onstage and I also block out the time I'll need onstage for various setups.

"I usually go over the contracts that have been signed with the actors. For instance, I check things like dressing rooms. Sometimes, actors are given the contractual right to have their own dressing rooms, but the theater just doesn't have enough to accommodate all of them. Or I make sure that a hair rider [a standard clause which gives management the right to alter, color, or change an actor's hair] is attached if the show is going to have wigs or hair changes. I find I must be aggressive about everything. Everyone wants to postpone things until a decision must be forced. I feel that a large part of my job is to anticipate these negative decisions—the decisions that no one is going to like—and to make sure that they are made.

"As it gets closer to rehearsal, I get a prop list done. I ask the director which props he will want during rehearsal and if necessary, I get them built. [You can't use the same props on stage as are used during rehearsal. It's a union rule.] I also hire my assistants, something I am now almost always permitted to do. It depends upon the size of the show, but usually there is a stage manager and at least one assistant stage manager. I now have a team of people with whom I like to work and they are very skilled.

"I also try to hire or at least have some say over who heads up the crews [stagehands who actually work on the show setting up scenery, props, running the lights, and so forth]. I'm the one who will have to work with them and, again, under a certain time deadline. The time pressure is always killing. Ultimately, the director will always take as much time as he can; the designer will always overdesign in order to cover himself; the music will keep being changed. And there is always that brick wall of the first preview date.

"Before rehearsals begin, I call each actor individually. I tell him what to expect, whether there will be any press there on the first day, and in general try to establish a rapport. This is important, because there won't be much time later and I'll be working with the actors after opening as well as during rehearsal. I also like actors to feel comfortable when they walk into rehearsal. It's a tense time for them.

"When rehearsals actually begin, I continue working with the designers and the shops. But I also start working with the director. I take down all the blocking and start getting the promptbook together."

The promptbook is the script that will be used by the stage manager in calling the show. It is also the beginning of the script that will be published and then sold to other producing organizations. The idea is to make it theoretically possible to re-create the original production. There are stage directions, descriptions of the sets and costumes, and even short remarks about the characters' emotions. The technical plots, which are breakdowns of the individual design elements of the play, are often added as well. There is a scenery plot that lists the scenery and how the sets operate; a property plot that lists each prop and when and where it is placed onstage; a lighting plot that lists all lighting equipment, its placement, and when and how it is used; a costume plot that lists each costume for each actor, including accessories, makeup, and wigs; and a sound plot that lists equipment, sound effects, and cues.

"If the director says that he wants to accomplish a certain thing, I try to figure out a way of getting it done. Sometimes I have to tell him that something is impossible. I'm very careful about physical safety. I see myself as the liaison between the actors and management, although some stage managers see themselves more as management. But I'm in the actor's union and I feel that management has enough people looking out for its interests. So, if anything, I'm probably too strict about safety, rehearsal time, and preparation time. But different stage managers have different feelings about these things.

"One of the things I like best about stage managing is that there is really no job description. It all depends upon the particular needs of the production. For instance, on *The First*, Martin Charnin was such a strong director that he didn't need any help organizing time or coping with actors. However, some directors need to be taken by the hand and told, 'Here's a block of time for this.'

"The thing about doing a show is that you must arrive at opening night. You have to do the show in front of an audience sometime. The producer tells you when that time is and you simply must be ready. Some directors can't manage to accomplish a certain amount of work in a limited amount of time. In that case, my job is to go to the director and say, 'Here is your schedule and this is what you are going to rehearse.' Usually, directors are glad to have that kind of stage manager. Some directors even want you to rehearse the company one day a week. Every show is different.

"Sometimes I must be more technically involved than at other times. Or sometimes it's more important for me to be dealing with personalities. Traditionally, stage managers must be political and take care of other people's egos. But again, it is the personalities of those in charge of the production that determine where my energies must go."

Once the show opens, the production stage manager becomes the director's representative at the theater. He is in charge of maintaining the show and also must make sure that the production runs smoothly at each performance.

"Stage managers always used to call the show. But today, especially with the 'heavy musicals,' you must have assistants who really know their stuff. As production stage manager, my job is not a technical one after opening. It is to give notes, recast when necessary, and keep the show in good shape. On a lot of musicals, the production stage manager doesn't call the show at all. But I always do it up through opening night, and then usually about three times a week. It's important for me to know the show and you can really only know it by calling it. I also find it a good way for me to keep in touch with the backstage crew. When a show is very technical, the relationship with the crew becomes especially important. On *The First* we had more stagehands than actors—thirty-five in all. Just running the backstage part of the show took three stage managers: someone on the book, one offstage left and one offstage right.

"There are an incredible number of things that must be checked before curtain. On *The First* the assistant stage managers did that and they were always checking plugs, connections, and all the moving parts of the platforms and winches. It's not that stagehands are inefficient, it's just that these heavy musicals have so many things that can go wrong technically that everyone must check and double-check."

In addition to making sure that the physical parts of production are in working order, the production stage manager must make sure that the actors are in good shape. He watches the show on a regular basis and gives notes to performers who are deviating from the performance. If there are any personal problems with actors, the stage manager is usually called upon to intercede. The production stage manager calls and directs the once-a-week understudy rehearsal and often directs cast replacements as well.

"I note about four times a week. When I'm not calling the show, I'm watching it. When I put new people into a show, I feel that there is a fine line between carrying out the director's intentions and just being a carbon copy. Each actor is different, and while I have an obligation to put someone in relatively the same place as the original actor, I do have to work with an actor who is assuming the role and help him perform his best."

The Musical Theater

Musicians

Musicians work primarily in the commercial theater including dinner theater, summer stock and tent shows, arena attractions, and, of course, Broadway musicals and their national and touring companies. Regional and not-for-profit theaters don't regularly produce musicals, although there are, of course, exceptions.

In the commercial theater, musicians must be members of the American Federation of Musicians. There are approximately 600 chapters or, as they are called, locals throughout the United States and Canada. A musician joins the local that has jurisdiction over the city or region in which he lives. In New York City musicians are members of Local 802, which has jurisdiction over all Broadway and off-Broadway theatrical work.

Although there is basic reciprocity among union locals, which permits musicians who are members of one local to work in another local's domain, this is not easily accomplished in the musical theater. Special waivers are required for non-Local 802 members to work in the New York theater and these waivers are not easy to come by. Usually, one must join Local 802 in order to work on Broadway or off-Broadway. This can be done after establishing a residence in New York City for a minimum of six months. For musicians who live in the New York City environs and whose actual residence comes under the jurisdiction of another local, dual membership is often permitted. Many people who work in the city commute from the suburbs or New Jersey, so a musician might be a member of his residence local and Local 802.

When a production travels, the musicians who travel with the production come under the jurisdiction of the union's national office. Under what is called a Pamphlet B, bus-and-truck companies and the musicians who travel with musical touring shows such as star packages, summer stock and arena attractions, and Broadway national companies can work even if they are not members of the local that covers the area in which the production is playing. In most cases, however, a show that is not doing one-night stands or split weeks travels only with a musical director, assistant musical director, and perhaps some key musicians. Musicians who are members of each area's local are then hired for the duration of the show's engagement.

Musicians are hired for the pit orchestra by a musical contractor. The contractor is hired by the producer or general manager and, working with the musical director, hires those who will play in the orchestra. In the theater the contractor holds a powerful position. A job as pit musician provides a steady income in a business in which a regular income is often difficult to achieve. Once hired, a pit musician is permitted to take off four performances a week and can often work out even longer absences from a show. This gives the musician the opportunity to do other concert, orchestra, or even touring work. Each musician has a sub, another musician who substitutes for him when he is unable to play. Although the musical director must approve all musicians' subs, being a sub is a good way to break into the orchestra pit.

Rehearsal Pianist

Rehearsal pianists accompany dancers and singers during rehearsals. Often the rehearsal pianist is employed for the run of a show. In addition to playing at preopening rehearsals, accompaniment is needed at weekly understudy rehearsals, brush-up rehearsals, cast replacement rehearsals, and rehearsals for national or touring companies. Sometimes, however, the assistant musical director handles rehearsals after opening.

This is a good entry job for keyboard players who hope to get into the pit orchestra. Keyboard players are often the last instrumentalists hired for the pit orchestra. The rehearsal pianist is, by that time, often indispensable to the production. He knows the score well and has worked with the company since the beginning of rehearsals. A rehearsal pianist who is versatile, skilled, able to work under pressure, and willing to take on extra tasks is not only valuable but frequently noticed by those who have input in selecting those who will join the production's permanent musical staff.

Audition Pianist

The audition pianist is hired by the casting director to accompany singers and performers who are auditioning for a role. Obviously, the audition pianist must be able to play in any key and sight-read with ease. A good audition pianist helps calm performers who are seeking parts and is invaluable to the entire casting process. In a production that has opened, the rehearsal pianist often plays for auditions that are held for cast replacements and additional companies.

Vocal Arranger

The vocal arranger takes the composer's basic melody and organizes it into a piece of vocal music with harmonies, structure, and rhythm. This is often done by the musical director, but if not, a vocal arranger is retained. How much actual work is necessary depends upon the composer. Some composers can only sing a melody and literally need someone to write down the music. Other composers bring a fairly complete work to rehearsal, with most of the arrangements set and in good shape.

The vocal arranger must represent the composer's musical concept. However, arrangers do have input into the actual sound of the music. Often, it is only during rehearsals that a decision is made to turn a musical number into a tango or rock sequence featuring chorus and soloists. The arranger takes the composer's original music and adapts it to the particular style that is to be used in the show.

Dance Arranger

The dance arranger works with the choreographer and rehearsal pianist in much the same way as the vocal arranger. However, there is much less leeway allowed in dance arrangements than for vocal ones. The dance arranger must be able to adapt the music to the particular needs of the dancers. For instance, a dancer can only hold certain positions for a limited length of time or do so many leaps. Rhythm and time must be exact and fit the specific steps performed and capabilities of the dancers.

Orchestrator

During rehearsals, only piano arrangements are used. The orchestrator takes these arrangements and sets the music for the various instruments of the orchestra. He starts working toward the middle of the rehearsal period and is responsible for the overall sound of the music. The orchestrator must work with aesthetic and practical considerations. He collaborates with the composer, director, and often the musical director as it is necessary that he understand the composer's musical and dramatic intentions.

The orchestrator must also know how many instruments will be playing the music. Pit musicians frequently play more than one instrument, but each musician gets paid extra money for each instrument played. The producer often limits the number of musicians and instruments in order to save money. The orchestrator must work around such limitations.

Musical Preparation

Among the least known of the musical theater's specialists are those who prepare the music. In a new musical, the music has never been performed. It has been written and composed solely for the show. Someone has to get the music into workable shape for the musical director, orchestra, and for the music publishers who will print and make possible its distribution and sale.

Mathilde Pincus has prepared the music for more than 150 shows, including *Evita, Dreamgirls, Nine, Sweeney Todd,* and *Peter Pan*. In 1976 she was awarded a special Tony Award for her outstanding contribution to the Broadway theater.

* * *

"I grew up in Philadelphia and played violin and viola from the time I was five years old. I studied at the Curtis Institute of Music. One day I was asked to copy the music for a show which was being done at the University of Pennsylvania. I thought I'd be very slow but I sort of knew what I was doing. I'd studied harmony, orchestrations, and had written scores. The conductor was very pleased with my work, and from that time on, when New York shows came to Philadelphia for their pre-Broadway tryouts, I often prepared the music. I worked with people like Cole Porter, Irving Berlin, and Aaron Copland.

"The work started to get fairly lucrative and I was flattered because people were saying, 'She's good, let's get her.' Pretty soon, I became so busy that I didn't have time to keep playing. In 1950 I came to New York and since that time I've worked with Jonathan Tunick, Stephen Sondheim, Hal Prince, John Kander, Sheldon Harnick, Angela Lansbury—almost everybody involved in the musical theater.

"We are called music copyists but we really aren't. I prefer the term music preparation. We prepare the music. Most people have no idea how music gets into the orchestra pit. Without us, a show couldn't get on. You can't do this by machine. Machines can't make changes and corrections. It must be done by people.

"Before rehearsal begins, the composer turns his songs over to us. They may be as fragmentary as a pencil sketch showing just the basic melodies and indicating harmonies. Sometimes they're like road maps. The composer uses symbols which we often have to decipher. They can mean 'raise this a fourth,' 'transpose that down a key,' 'repeat a fifth higher,' or any number of things. What we are doing is making a piano reduction, which is simply a score which can be played on the piano. It is what can be used at rehearsal by the rehearsal pianists and the musical director in order to teach the music. The arranger can work from this reduction as well. Some composers are marvelous musicians and write out fairly complete sets of music. Others, however, just write a lead sheet and need someone else to do all the chords. We are all highly trained musicians, so we can do whatever is necessary."

Pincus and her staff even have prepared the music from scratch. When they were working on *Sophisticated Ladies*, which utilizes Duke Ellington's original music, they had to listen to tapes and recordings of Ellington's own performances. Since so much of jazz is improvisational, many of Ellington's arrangements had never been formally transcribed. Literally taking the notes and transcribing them as they listened, Pincus and her staff wrote the rehearsal music. This was then orchestrated and recopied by them for all of the instruments.

When a show begins rehearsal, the music is taught to the performers. Refinements and changes are made and the songs are set. The music is then given to the orchestrator, who sets it for the various instruments that will comprise the pit orchestra. Orchestrators use special, large-size music copying paper that names each instrument to be used. Each instrumental part is scored separately in its indicated position on the paper. The copyist reads each part, following it all the way through, and writes a separate score for each instrument. This is called "extracting parts" and is the way in which each musician receives the music that he will play during the show. The copyist checks for possible errors in orchestration and is careful even to indicate page turns. Since most instruments are played with two hands, a musician must turn the page when there is a break in the music, which is not necessarily at the end of the page.

While these individual instrumental parts are being extracted and prepared, a piano reduction is prepared for the musical director. This piano reduction includes the piano part, vocal melody, and instrumental lines that the musical director must know while conducting the show. Certain cues are indicated, as well as any special instrumental patterns. Accuracy is crucial, and this is why good copyists are invaluable. As trained and exacting musicians, they not only catch mistakes but also implicitly understand when something in the music doesn't make sense. And since everything is always rushed and tense before an opening, mistakes and omissions are not uncommon.

The most intense period of music preparation is during previews or pre-Broadway out-of-town tryouts. During previews and tryouts, the show is performed before live audiences. Producers and directors have the opportunity to see what works and what doesn't. Changes are made, often on a daily basis. And if the show is in trouble, the changes can be radical, with new songs written, old material removed, and other songs revised or rewritten. A decision might be made to write a new song for the next day's performance. This means that it must be written, orchestrated, and copied for the orchestra.

"When we were doing *Merrily We Roll Along*, we got the song 'Rich and Happy' at three-thirty P.M. It was supposed to be in the show that evening. With *Sophisticated Ladies* we had changes at five-thirty P.M. that had to be in the show that night. Musicians would be cutting and pasting right before curtain time. We really must be involved in the show and must know what's going on. Everything changes constantly.

Whenever we make a change, we put a date on it so that we can keep track of what was done and when. Many times, people will put a change in and decide to go back to the way the number was originally or combine various changes.

"We go out of town with a show when it is doing a pre-Broadway tryout. [The exception to this is Los Angeles. There are talented copyists there, so if the office has a show in Los Angeles, Pincus or one of her staff goes out to supervise local copyists. In any other city though, a staff member goes out with the show.] We take a printing machine with us and loads of other equipment and material. [The machine employs a blueprint process like that used by architectural firms. The copyist writes on an onionskin drafting paper that is the master. When placed on light-sensitive paper under a high-intensity light and run through a developer, music is then actually imprinted on paper.] We take our own machine because it is impossible to get anyone to do this kind of duplicating on a weekend or late at night. We get terrible deadlines. No one takes no for an answer in this business. The only way they do is when you tell them the cost. Everything is a crisis before opening.

"You usually get into a situation where a new number is going into the show. The composer is writing frantically, and every two minutes the arranger or musical director comes in and hands us new material. People just get frantic. We usually set up banquet tables in this beautiful room we've taken, and within minutes it's a mess . . . paper, printing materials, tapes, and all our other supplies.

"The other thing we've learned is always to have cash for tips and emergencies. We were going out with a show in Chicago last winter and went to the airport only to discover that our flight had been cancelled because there was a blizzard in

Chicago and our plane couldn't land. There was a rehearsal the next morning and we had all the music with us. We ran to Penn Station from the airport with all our big trunks and bags and did manage to get on the overnight train to Chicago. It cost us two hundred fifty dollars just to get on that train."

Pincus and her staff compile what she calls her "trademark," which are complete piano reduction scores for all shows. Painstakingly done by hand, these "green books," as they are called because of their green covers, contain each song in the show, any songs that were dropped from the show, and even copies of original billing pages and cast lists. Chorus, orchestral instruments, rhythms, and harmonies are all indicated in these transcriptions. They are collector's items given to the composer, and are an accurate record of the original music and scoring of most of Broadway's major musicals.

Pincus and her staff also work on the recording of a new musical.

"We help set the session up. A recording doesn't necessarily reflect the show accurately. The orchestrations may be expanded, and of course, dance numbers and transitional music are cut. Years ago, before copying machines, we would get the music from the show around eleven P.M. when the curtain came down. A whole crew would come in and we'd work all night making the cuts and putting in the additions. Then when the recording session was over, we had to go back and restore the music to its original state. Now, as soon as the show opens and we know the music is set, we photocopy all the parts, do the cuts, and make any changes. We then have a complete recording set. This saves a lot of money on overtime to say nothing of people's health.

"This work is very demanding but so exciting. There is a

great personal relationship that we have with most of the composers and we are involved with the actual creation of the music . . . the part that lives."

Musical Director

As conductor of the pit orchestra, the musical director is the most visible member of the production's musical team. With the stage manager, the musical director maintains the show as set by its creators after opening and during the run.

Musical directors are highly trained musicians. They are usually proficient in several instruments and skilled in improvisation, composition, and arranging. They must work well with people, inspiring the trust and confidence of the performers and the respect of those in the orchestra. The musical director literally holds the production together, coordinating action, voice, and instruments during performance.

Yolanda Segovia is a Broadway musical director. She is currently conducting *Dreamgirls*.

* * *

"I was born and raised in Tulsa, Oklahoma. I studied the piano but quit when I got to high school. I attended Oklahoma State as a pre-med major, but since I wasn't sure whether or not I actually wanted to go on to medical school, I decided to get all the required courses out of the way and then take some music courses. I ended up as a performance major in piano.

"During my senior year, I auditioned for the graduate program in music at Michigan State and was accepted. Each summer I had been playing for Six Flags, a chain of amusement parks. Each park had an elaborate musical review with an orchestra of about twenty-five people. It was a union job so I was getting union wages.

"The summer after graduation, I was working at Six Flags over Texas. I didn't really have my heart set on graduate school and decided to stay in Texas. I worked as a pit musician for a chain of dinner theaters and became musical director. After that, I started to do club work in Dallas, singing and playing. I also continued to accompany singers."

While attending a musical theater workshop near Dallas, Segovia met Pat Birch, choreographer of the Broadway production of *Grease*. Birch suggested that Segovia come to New York.

"I came to New York and plunked my money down so I could join Local 802. But in large cities, you have to be a resident for six months before you can work union jobs. So I had the hassle of finding all sorts of odd jobs. I'd leave my name at rehearsal studios in case someone needed vocal coaching or an accompanist. I played a lot of auditions, particularly *Grease* auditions because of Pat Birch. Suddenly, I was working a lot. I worked with The Acting Company and got to know Mathilde Pincus, the copyist. She recommended me for a job as rehearsal pianist at *Dancin'*.

"For *Dancin'* I had to play all kinds of music—rock, classical, jazz. There were also a lot of brush-up and understudy rehearsals. Usually a show only rehearses understudies once a week, but *Dancin'* was such a technical show, there were more.

"I had been asked to join the pit orchestra but decided not to. Some rehearsal pianists do play in the pit, but it is exhausting to do both, particularly on such an active show. There's a lot of work to do after a show opens—brush-ups, understudy rehearsals, auditions for national companies and replacements. I even went out of town to play rehearsals for the Boston company.

"I was then asked to play rehearsals for *King of Hearts*. We went out of town for a pre-Broadway tryout and I ended up playing both rehearsals and in the pit. Because I was doing preproduction work, I had to start work about two hours earlier than the cast. So I'd work from about nine A.M. until six P.M. and then run and play in the show. I really knew the show better than anyone at that point.

"Meanwhile, the musical director just wasn't working out. He was fired and left the same day, without waiting for his replacement. There was a real commotion about who was going to lead that night's performance. Finally, the general manager came up to me and said, 'Yolanda, you're going to conduct tonight.'

"Well, I knew the music from playing during the day and I also knew the orchestrations from playing at each performance. I was very nervous beforehand, but as soon as I got in front of the orchestra, I felt fine. As a musician, I knew what I wanted to hear and I got the results I wanted. It went off very well and when we came into New York, I became the assistant musical director. [The assistant musical director is the back-up/understudy to the musical director. Often the assistant conducts the show once a week, so that the musical director can listen to the orchestra to ascertain how the entire show sounds in various parts of the theater. The assistant musical director is usually a member of the pit orchestra.]

"Unfortunately, *King of Hearts* didn't last too long and I returned to *Dancin'*, playing keyboard in the pit. I moved on to play keyboard for *They're Playing Our Song* and ended up assistant musical director. During that time, I started doing industrial shows, recording work, and vocal coaching. I like it when a show runs, because I can do other work during the day. Playing in the pit is just not that fulfilling and I need to do other things as well."

Segovia left *They're Playing Our Song* to become rehearsal pianist for *Perfectly Frank*. She became musical director, but the production closed within a few weeks. As Local 802 doesn't permit musicians to quit one show in order to join another and then return to the same position in the former show, she was unable to rejoin *They're Playing Our Song* until a new position opened. It was while she was playing piano in the pit orchestra that she got a call from Michael Bennett asking to speak with her about his new show *Dreamgirls*.

"He said that my recommendations were very good, but that he wanted to try me out as assistant musical director. I said, 'No. Hire me as musical director and if you like my work, fine. But if you don't, you can fire me.' It turned out that was what he wanted to hear. He just didn't want to have to fire anyone. So *Dreamgirls* became the first show on which I was hired as full musical director from the beginning."

Normally, the musical director is hired and begins work well in advance of rehearsal. Working with the composer, the musical director oversees the preparation of the music so that it is ready for rehearsal. Since the musical director will teach the music to the actors and chorus during rehearsal, the musical director makes sure that vocal arrangements are satisfactory and that the rehearsal pianists have scores from which to accompany singers and dancers.

This requires a tremendous amount of organization and collaboration, all of which is coordinated by the musical director. Since several creative people (arrangers and orchestrator) are working with the composer's music, and the director is establishing the actual context in which the music will be used and determining style and mood, someone must make sure that everyone is operating under the same musical assumptions and along the same track. There can be problems when too many people are involved. The musical director must anticipate these problems and refocus directions when necessary.

In addition, the musical director must organize the actual flow of paper: from arranger to pianist and back to arranger, and from arranger to orchestrator and on to the copyist. He must also make sure that the music is ready on time and in the right place, either at rehearsal or in front of the orchestra. There is a lot of detail work during preproduction and rehearsal.

"During preproduction, I am getting the music ready. You don't go to the actors on the first day of rehearsal and say, 'Let's try this.' That's wasting everyone's time, and time is the one thing you never have enough of. During those six weeks of rehearsal, you should be refining what has already been established before rehearsals even begin.

"During preproduction and rehearsal, I am basically a facilitator and organizer. I make sure that the arrangements make sense and that the composer's musical concept is being adhered to. A lot of conductors do the vocal arrangements themselves, but I don't like to. Not only does it mean that I have to go home each night and work on arrangements, but I feel I need all the time I can get to keep on top of everyone— the arranger, the orchestrator, and the copyist. I always have to know the current state of the music.

"I teach the vocals to both leads and chorus. During rehearsal, we change and create a lot. If there is someone who can do something special, for instance an actor with an incredible vocal range or a dancer who can do an intricate leap, material is often changed for them. Initially, so much is based on the capabilities and strengths of the performers. If a new person joins the cast, keys are changed and sometimes orchestrations must be revised.

"When the number is set, the orchestrator comes in. He is expanding the musical concept for twenty or so instruments. We discuss instruments and the director talks about what he wants to accomplish through the music. After the orchestrator has written all the parts for the orchestra, the music goes to the copyists, who copy each part out by hand and prepare it for the orchestra. That's the last step and involves extremely skilled work. If it isn't accurate, you end up wasting a lot of time during orchestra rehearsal. Certain copyists just have a way of looking at the music and implicitly knowing what it means. They know how to put it down on paper in the easiest way for a musician or musical director to read it. They are just invaluable."

The musical director is also involved in hiring musicians. Although the musical contractor actually hires the musicians, the musical director works closely with him.

"I have input into the musician-hiring process. If there are some people I particularly want or don't want, I tell the contractor. I tell him what the most important chairs will be in the orchestra. It's important to have a good relationship with the contractor, because he can make your life a lot easier. He takes care of orchestra payrolls, handles union business, and can mediate between you and a musician if there are any problems.

"I hold the first orchestra rehearsal about three days before the first preview. We rent a studio and the orchestra assembles. There are only about six hours to go through the entire show the first time, and then the company comes in and just sings along with the orchestra. It's the first time they've heard what the music really sounds like and that's always thrilling."

Once the show opens, the stage manager and musical director are the representatives of the show's creators who are at the theater for each performance. Both are in charge of running the show and maintaining the production. Like the stage manager, the musical director gives notes to performers and must cope with performance issues and problems for the run of the show.

"I'm there for every performance and I get all the complaints about the music, sound, and performances. I give a lot of notes, both to the cast and the sound people. Sometimes the sound mix has been off, or I've heard a sound that shouldn't be there. I want to know what I heard.

"I have to keep the cast together musically and keep the orchestra sounding good. Sometimes I think that musical performers are a special breed. So many times I'm dealing with people's insecurities. I'll tell one of the performers that something isn't right and make a suggestion. I get a lot of excuses from the cast, and often people will say, 'I can't,' when I've told them I want them to do something. You have to make sure that your cast understands that you want them to do something that will make them look their best. You have no vengeance towards them. It's for them.

"*Dreamgirls* is a fun show. It's all music, which means we don't spend a lot of time hanging around listening to scenes. About the only problem I have with the orchestra is that most of them have known me as a piano player, playing with them in the pit. Sometimes, when I get serious, they don't take me seriously. For instance, if I tell them not to wear jeans, it's hard to get them to listen to me. When I was playing in the pit, I was the first one in jeans or in colors which you're not supposed to wear. I sometimes have this feeling of 'Who am I to be telling people things like that?' But basically, this is a really good orchestra and everyone really wants to do their best. People work well together and help each other out, musically and personally."

Theatrical Design

Set, costume, and lighting designers create the physical environment in which the actors perform their roles. They translate the playwright and director's vision into concrete, visual terms. Sound designers facilitate the director's aural and acoustic sense of the production.

Designers work in commercial and not-for-profit theater, although sound design is almost exclusively limited to the commercial musical theater. Off-Broadway and regionally, sound technicians handle special effects and amplification if and when it is used in production.

In the commercial theater, set, costume, and lighting designers are members of the United Scenic Artists (USA), Local 829. Entry requirements include an entrance examination held at union headquarters, an interview at which the portfolio is evaluated, and a home project. This is a very difficult union in which to gain admission and designers often take the exam several times before passing. Although those who design for not-for-profit theater do not have to be union members, the USA has created minimum wage scales and conditions which are adhered to by the regional theaters.

There is no union for sound designers. However, most join the International Alliance of Theatrical Stage Employees

138

(IATSE) in order to work in the theater as sound operators during performance of their shows.

Set Design

The set designer is responsible for the actual physical environment of the production. Working with the director, the set designer plans the scenery and is responsible for its execution and installation in the theater. Sets can range from the extremely complex, involving complicated mechanical equipment, to a simple backdrop against which the play is performed.

The set designer translates the vision of the playwright and director into a concrete design. To do so requires both specific drafting, artistic, and architectural skills and creative sensibilities.

John Lee Beatty has designed the sets for numerous regional and off-Broadway productions. He has been resident set designer at Circle Repertory Company. On Broadway, he designed the sets for *Ain't Misbehavin'*, *Hide and Seek*, *Fifth of July*, and *Talley's Folly*, for which he won a Tony Award.

* * *

"I suppose you could say I've been a set designer since I was seven. I grew up in Southern California and my parents made the mistake of taking me to see Mary Martin in *Peter Pan* when it was in Los Angeles before going to Broadway. That did it. I went home and took out my construction paper and shoe boxes and started making sets for *Peter Pan*. I suppose that deep in my heart I knew that there were other plays, but I don't remember being conscious of any others until we went to Europe for a year. I saw a lot of theater there and realized that there was more to the theater than just *Peter Pan.*

"When we returned home, I started making sets out of small blocks and actually built a miniature theater in our garage using small fly systems and pulleys. I had about thirty-five miniature sets at home, and all through school I was directing and designing plays.

"I went to Brown University and majored in English literature. I worked on productions there and designed sets and costumes. I even taught myself to sew on a sewing machine using an instruction book. My summers were spent working in stock, including, after my junior year, the College Light Opera Company in Falmouth, Massachusetts. It was wonderful. We did nine shows in as many weeks. I just built, painted, and designed scenery all the time. I was killing myself but I'd never been happier.

"When I went back to Brown for my senior year, I had my first course in technical theater. I learned the tools you use in the theater; how to build a flat; how to mix paints; color theory; drafting; three-dimensional visualization; and basic lighting design. I really hadn't thought about what I was going to do after graduation. I had thought about being an English teacher, but the man who taught the technical course at Brown had gone to Yale and he suggested I apply. So I did and was accepted. I really had no awareness of what it meant. I had come from an academic family and Yale was certainly a nice name and my parents were pleased.

"I started at Yale, and Ming Cho Lee was my teacher. My first assignment was to do a sketch for *Medea.* It was tense for me, because it was the first time I had ever been with other designers and Lee was the first person I had ever known who was a working designer. I got my first taste of competition and discovered that I loved it. Suddenly, my work started getting better and I decided that I was going to be a designer and nothing was going to stop me.

"We had to do one design a week, which included a color sketch, the floor plan of a set, and a rendering. We'd often go to New York and see a theater and then be assigned a project for that particular theater. Color sketches were the most difficult for me. You portray the design in watercolor form and try to render it so you can see the light and actual modeling—the way it will look onstage. I worked on shows at Yale and during the summer did more stock.

"I had heard about the exam necessary to get into the union [United Scenic Artists]. One of my teachers at Yale had been the head artist in charge at Nolan Scenery Studios, which was a large scenic house. I loved his work and I loved scene painting. But I knew that to be able to work in a scenic shop, I would have to be a union member. I applied to take the exam for membership, took it, and passed the first time.

"I had interviewed in Washington, D.C., at the Arena Stage and at the Folger, hoping that they would hire me to do a show. But they didn't, and I decided to come to New York City. I knew that as a union member I could always get a job as a scenic artist, which paid very well. When I got to New York, a friend of mine recommended me for his job, which he was leaving, as assistant to designer Douglas Schmidt. I was hired and it turned out to be a wonderful experience.

"I sewed, bought props, looked for furniture, helped with the drafting, helped with painter's elevations, worked on scenic sketches, went to the theater with him, and worked on props. I would take drawings out to be photostated, did research, built models, and even went out of town with him when he was working. I answered the phone and discovered that it is amazing how much you can learn even from that. I discovered how everything worked on the business end, from how he got paid and banking, to all of the actual details involved in really working as a set designer. He was very generous about telling me everything—how things worked, who was nice and was not nice, who to trust and who not to—all those really invaluable things.

"I had gone over to the Manhattan Theatre Club because the general manager was a friend of mine from Brown and Yale days. It was, in those days, a very small operation, with just four people on staff. I did my first off-Broadway show there and then heard that the Queens Playhouse was looking for a cheap designer. They were doing a season and wanted a designer who was in the union but who was willing and able to do a lot of work and function as scenic artist as well. I was hired and on the third show, *Come Back, Little Sheba*, worked with Marshall Mason, who was directing. We worked very well together and he asked me to come and design his first show at Circle Repertory Company that fall.

"I started doing a lot of work for the Manhattan Theatre Club and Circle Rep. Soon, I got too busy to work for Doug Schmidt anymore. All the work I had done in college and in stock really began paying off, because I knew how to do things fast and cheap. I also knew how to paint and build—all technical things. Because of my work with Doug, I knew how to buy furniture and where to find things. It all started to come together.

"My first regional job was with the Seattle Repertory Theatre, and then I finally got to work at the Arena Stage. During my second season at Circle Rep, their production of *Knock, Knock* moved to Broadway. I had designed it and the whole move turned out to be a disaster. But it was a Broadway credit.

"My second Broadway show was *The Innocents*, which Harold Pinter was directing. They wanted a young designer and asked to see my portfolio. They didn't want to see me and I was asked to drop my portfolio off at Pinter's hotel. I didn't like that too much, but I did it and went for a walk. When I came back, I was told that Pinter wanted to meet me. I went upstairs and he asked me if I would like to work with him on the show. Well, of course I said yes. And as I was walking down the street after meeting him, I started to cry. I was so happy and flattered. I had been chosen by Harold Pinter solely on the basis of my portfolio. The play was not a success, but I was pleased with my work and I started getting awfully busy. I think there was a period of time when I did sixteen shows in one year—regional, Broadway, and off-Broadway. I was holding on for dear life. I started to get depressed and my health started to suffer. I've learned since then. Now, I pick and choose a lot more. I'm also trying to cut down on my regional work. For the past three years, one third of my nights have been spent out of town and there have been a lot of day trips as well, which are exhausting."

When designing a set, the first thing the designer does is collaborate with the director. The director has the final responsibility of piecing together all the elements into a unified whole. They must mutually arrive at answers to such questions as: In what time period will the production be set? How elaborate will the set be? Will it be a single, standing set throughout the play or an elaborate combination of sets requiring technological support? What is the basic feel of the set? Is it to be stark? Eclectic? What will the actors need to be able to do within the context of the set?

"I love working with the director. I like to get involved in the problems unique to the theater. Basically, though, I still work out of a paper bag. I have the same drawing table I've always had and the same T-square. I only hire an assistant when I'm doing Broadway, and then usually for only a few weeks. He helps me build and can look for furniture and props—the same kind of stuff I did for Schmidt.

"I draft the show and then we draw up plans like an architect. Often I build a model [to give a three-dimensional reality to the concept], and then, assuming everyone likes it, we have a bid session. Maybe six shops will come in and look at the model. A few days later, they present bids. I have some say in all this. Perhaps I've had a bad time with one shop or a particularly good time with another. I might know that one particular shop has a very good man to do the woodwork, and this is a show which will require a lot of woodwork. So we don't always choose the shop on the basis of the least expensive bid, although the most expensive one never seems to get the work.

"While the set is being built, I go to the shop at least ten or twelve times. The guys are nice and I know them now. I don't change my mind a lot, but I like to make sure that it's all being done the way I want. If you have to make changes when you're in the theater, it costs a lot more money.

"When I'm working at a regional theater, I make a minimum of three trips. Usually, the director comes to New York and we have our initial talks here. But if I haven't seen the theater, I go out. My second trip is after I've done all the drawings and sketches. I spend a few days picking out basic pieces that we might have to buy. [Regional theaters often have their own scenic construction shops and scenery is constructed on the premises. Because scenery is usually the most expensive component of production, most regional theaters have basic pieces of scenery that can be used in more than one production.] I then come back midway through the construction to make sure that everything is going all right and then make another trip during the last week to oversee the last part of the building, painting, and detail work. I also make any changes that must be done at that point."

There are, of course, differences in working for Broadway and off-Broadway and regional theater.

"Broadway is terrifying in the beginning. There are all sorts of anxieties. You're really afraid you're going to mess up. [This is especially true after doing so much work alone and now having to rely on others to do the actual construction, under what can be difficult circumstances for novice designers. A beginning designer working for the first time in a scenic shop with a big-budget Broadway show where everyone is under pressure and increasingly worried as opening night approaches, is in a tense situation, to say the least.] Will it cost too much to put up? Will it fit into the theater? Is it fireproof? Will the producer really like it? You just keep asking yourself those questions."

The stakes aren't so high in not-for-profit theater and the producing rationale clearer. On Broadway, the goal is to make money. Regionally, the play is intrinsic to the continuance of the theater and is part of the artistic purpose of the institution. The ingenuity of the set designer is tested in different ways, and the budgets, of course, aren't nearly as big. The feel is very different.

"I like to work with people on their way up. And it's very important for me to work on what I think are good plays. That means I still do a lot of off-Broadway and some regional theater. If I don't like a show, I won't do it."

Costume Design

The costume designer plans and executes the costumes for the production. Costumes may be purchased at department or specialty stores, rented from costume supply houses, or actually constructed at costume shops. In all cases, the costume designer, in collaboration with the director, is responsible for each piece of clothing worn by the actors in a show.

The costume designer must know design, fabric, and color. He must also understand how the onstage movements will affect the costume. Special circumstances, such as quick offstage changes, must be taken into consideration when designing the costumes. Unlike the other designers, the costume designer has a personal relationship with the lead actors in a production. Costumes are very important to actors. As part of their stage character, costumes must feel comfortable both emotionally and physically to the actors who wear them.

Jennifer von Mayrhauser has been resident designer for Circle Repertory Company. She has designed for regional theater, and on Broadway she designed costumes for *Da, Special Occasions, Talley's Folly, Knock, Knock,* and *Beyond Therapy.*

* * *

"I grew up in New Haven, Connecticut. I always loved the theater and started working as an apprentice in summer stock when I was sixteen. At first I wanted to be an actress, because it never occurred to me that I could do anything else in the theater. I went to Northwestern University as a theater major. I still thought I'd be an actress, but I took design courses as well. At Northwestern they just worked you to the ground and if you survived, you graduated.

"I had gotten a scholarship to go to Columbia University to study acting, but I decided not to go and took all the money I had and went to Europe for six months. When I returned, I came to New York to look for work. A friend of mine from Northwestern was working on a show at St. Clement's Church, and I ended up working as a sound technician on the production. From there I worked on a movie as an assistant director, which meant that I did nothing but pick up props and go on errands for people.

"When that was over, I went for an interview at the New York Shakespeare Festival, hoping to get a job in their prop department. I was told that there were no openings in props, but that the costume department needed someone. I went to work there and was placed in the armor department. [The New York Shakespeare Festival presents free plays in New York's Central Park each summer. Although in the past few years playwrights other than Shakespeare have been presented, in the early 1970s the Central Park productions were classical Shakespearian presentations. The Shakespeare Festival maintains its own costume shop, and costumes for the Central Park productions are made there.] There were tons of people working for practically no money. That summer I learned that I had a talent for dyeing, painting, and color. People began to think that I was a costume painter, and I actually managed to get a job as one. I really didn't know what I was doing, but I just did what I was told and it worked out.

"At that point I really got very involved with costumes and decided that if I was going to work with costumes, the only way to do it was to be a designer. So I went to Lester Polakov's at night [Lester Polakov's Studio and Forum of Stage Design] and also took drawing lessons at the New School. Through recommendations, I was able to get jobs assisting costume designers. I worked for Carrie Robbins and Santo Loquasto and learned a lot from them. I shopped, dyed, took notes, swatched fabrics—all the things you must know. During that time, I worked on some showcases and then, in 1972, a friend of mine who is a set designer and with whom I had worked recommended me to Marshall Mason at the Circle

Repertory Company. My friend was designing the sets for a new show, *Prodigal*, and thought that I might be able to do the costumes. Marshall agreed to let me, and from there I started designing at Circle Rep.

"That turned out to be very fortunate for me. Circle Rep was just beginning to get recognition as an innovative theater company in New York. Frankly, being associated with Circle Rep gave me a lot of visibility, and I started to get regional and off-Broadway work. By 1975 I decided to stop assisting designers. I think that if you're a really good assistant, you can get too associated with someone and typed as an assistant. That can be a problem, so I felt it was time to work on my own completely.

"At Circle Rep, I worked very hard. Now, I don't have the energy or strength to do what I did then. I was given two hundred fifty dollars a show and would just wing it. I'd find things, get friends to let me borrow clothing of theirs, and often literally patch things together. If I was doing a period show, I'd beg friends of mine who were good drapers to come and help, and then we'd sew the costumes ourselves.

"While I was at Circle Rep, I did costumes for a number of other off-Broadway shows. I joined the United Scenic Artists when I was asked to design the costumes for a television film and had to be in the union to do it. I had worked very hard on my sketching and had taken lots of courses and classes. Fortunately, I passed the first time."

Von Mayrhauser now designs primarily for the theater and television. She maintains a studio and, depending upon how many projects she is involved in at any one time, has up to two assistants working with her.

"When I'm called for a show, the first thing I want to know are the dates, who is directing, what the budget is, and then I ask to read the script. Budget is very important. If I'm told the budget is a certain amount, I take that very seriously and stick to it. If I feel I can't, I have to be specific about why I won't be able to. Sometimes, I know that I cannot do a show for the amount of money involved, given the time that we have. I have to turn the project down in that case. If there's not enough money to do it right, it doesn't pay to do the project and it would only make me look bad.

"If I decide to do the show, I meet with the director and then with the actors. The relationship between actors and the costume designer is very important. If they trust me, that's half the battle. We talk about character; I like to know how the actor feels about the person he is portraying and any strong feelings the actor might have about clothes—what he likes or doesn't like. Then, after the director and I, hopefully, have a common understanding about the costumes, I go home and sketch. Sometimes, if I've worked with the director before and we have a good relationship and the clothes are modern, I don't bother sketching. We just start shopping.

"If the show is set in a specific period, I do research. I look at old photographs, magazines, and paintings. If I'm designing old dresses, I might go to the Metropolitan Museum of Art and look at the costume collection. A lot of those dresses aren't put together the way we would do it today, and I like to find out how they are constructed. I do the research myself because I like to immerse myself in the particular period. No matter what the time period is, I consider the character a real person and I design for people. That kind of concentration helps me understand just who the character is that I'm dressing.

"Recently, I worked on *Special Occasions*, which starred Suzanne Pleshette and Richard Mulligan. I was able to go to the preproduction meetings that the director held with the set designer, which is really good. I knew what the set designer was doing and we could work closely together on the concept. It's very rare to have that kind of time with a show. I talked with Suzanne on the phone in November, while she was still in California, and met Richard in New York. Both came to New York in December and we talked more specifically about character and clothing preferences then.

"Richard's clothes were not a problem. They were purchased and just had to be fitted. Suzanne's clothes, however, were different. There were a lot of costumes, and twelve changes, some of them very quick, were required. The action in the play spanned a decade, from the 1970s to the 1980s, so subtle differences in style were called for. Half of Suzanne's costumes were purchased and the other half were built.

"I did sketches of those that were going to be made for her. Because she is a star and had very strong and very good ideas about clothes, we worked closely together. For some shows, when I sketch I prepare finished, beautifully painted pieces of artwork. In this case, I did pretty sketches but they were loose pencil designs. I did it that way so Suzanne could add things to the basic design if she wanted to. She knows a great deal about clothing and had a lot of input. Most of the time, particularly if a play is done in modern dress, actors contribute. They must be comfortable in the costume. I try to keep the relationship very open."

When the sketches are completed, the designer shows them to the director and producer. Often, they are shown to the actors as well. After adjustments or revisions, the designer gets bids from the costume shops that make the costumes for the theater. Once the shop is selected, costume construction begins.

"The shop makes bids on the basis of my description and the sketches. I usually do it on a casual basis and feel out the shop. I know what I'm looking for, and often the kind of clothes we are making determines which shop I want for the job. When I was doing *Special Occasions,* we had some difficult clothes to make. They had to be well made and look very beautiful. But they also had to be trick clothes, rigged for fast changes. In this case, I just took the clothes to one shop. I was dealing with a star who would need attention and I wanted people who I knew would make beautiful clothes for a good price. I knew that this particular shop had the right atmosphere for Suzanne, and indeed, she loved the place, felt in good hands, and was very happy with the clothes."

Costume shops have a reputation of being difficult places for designers who are just starting out.

"You have to learn the politics of being in a shop. There is a love/hate relationship between the designer and the shop people. You're always under scrutiny and, sometimes, the shops sort of test you. Perhaps, you've done a rough sketch. They'll say that you should make it more complete, although they can follow it perfectly well. But I'm the person whose head is on the chopping block. One thing you learn as a designer is that when you work with directors, actors, and shop people, you can't let your ego get in the way. Basically, though, I've been treated well."

In the costume shops, there are many specialists. The people who work in the shops are members of the International Ladies Garment Workers Union, of which there is a special theatrical division. There are buyers who are experts on fabric. If the designer doesn't do it herself, they select the fabric which will be used for the costume. Dyers change fabric color when necessary and drapers make the pattern that will be used in the actual construction of the costume. The seamstress sews the costume together and a fitter performs fittings on the actor. Finishers and trimmers add final touches and decorations to the costume.

"While the fabric is being selected and dyed, if necessary, the draper does what is called a muslin. The muslin is a mock-up of the costume and is also used as the pattern. This way, you can know what the costume will look like without cutting into the good fabric. For instance, when we were making a chiffon gown for Suzanne, we used cheap chiffon and an inexpensive lining fabric for the muslin of that dress. You make changes on the muslin so that, hopefully, you won't have to make major alterations on the costume itself.

"When the muslin is finished, the actor comes in for a first fitting. At that point, basic adjustments are made. The neckline may be changed, sleeves shortened, or any other necessary structural changes performed. This fitting is very important. It is the first time you can really see whether a particular costume is going to work. The second, and often final fitting, is done with the real fabric. The director and producer often come to the second fitting. During this entire process, from fabric selection to final fitting, I work out of an office in the costume shop. That way, I am there throughout the growth of the costume.

"I am involved in the entire look of the character. I work with the hair stylist or wigmaker. I show them sketches and we talk about the kind of feeling we are trying to convey. I also talk to the actor about the character in terms of makeup. Unlike television and film, where costume, makeup, and hair responsibilities are often divided among several people, in the theater you design the whole look.

"Before the costume leaves the shop and goes to the theater, I meet with the wardrobe mistress who will be responsible for the clothes. I give her and the stage manager a costume plot [which is a list of each costume and accessory, indicating exactly when it is to be used in the production] and tell her how each costume must be cared for—whether it should be dry-cleaned, hand-washed, etc. You'd be surprised what sometimes happens to costumes. It's terrible when they are not cared for correctly."

Designers who work regionally are unable to maintain the same involvement throughout the design process as they can when working in New York. Usually, the designer meets with the show's director, either in New York or at the regional theater, to discuss the production and its costumes. The designer travels to the theater to present the sketches and once they are approved, the theater's costume shop begins construction. The designer then makes several additional trips, one for each fitting and then for dress rehearsal. This kind of schedule can be grueling. However, Von Mayrhauser says: "In regional theater the costume shops are wonderful. Usually, they're only working on one show at a time and they both care a lot and have a lot of time. They tend to do beautiful work."

Lighting Design

Stage lighting as a real design element in the theater is relatively recent. Plays have required illumination since the advent of indoor theater, but it was only during the 1943–44 season, when *Brigadoon* listed a lighting designer as part of its artistic staff, that lighting became an integral part of the creative process. Only in 1970 did the annual Tony Awards begin to include a lighting design category. Today, lighting design is as much a part of the theater as set and costume design.

Computer technology has made lighting effects practically infinite in their possibilities. Furthermore, the population at large is aware of lighting in ways not even imagined two decades ago. Dimmers and track lighting, formerly only available at high cost and used primarily for commercial installation, are now purchased at reasonable prices and routinely used in the home to create different moods.

Stage lighting fulfills many functions. At its simplest, it illuminates the stage so that the audience can see what is happening. At its most subtle, it can establish mood and atmosphere. Stage lighting can provide information necessary to the story line of a show. For instance, time and place—dawn, sunset, night, weather—can be indicated by lights. Lighting can highlight an event or character so that an action taking place within the context of other events stands out, however subtly, to the audience. It can change colors, alter appearances, be soothing or garish. Stage lighting determines the quality of the theatrical experience as much as the more quantifiable design elements of sets and costumes.

Ken Billington has designed extensively for Broadway, opera, dance, television, Las Vegas production shows, and many star acts.

* * *

"All I ever wanted to be was a Broadway lighting designer. I grew up in Harrison, New York, and from the time I pulled the curtain for the first-grade play, I somehow knew what I wanted to do. I ran lights for school theater productions and worked with the local community theater. My family went to New York City frequently and we saw plays, operas, and movies. I was always fascinated by the lighting.

"Harrison had a good school system, but nobody knew anything about theater. It was a dirty word. When I announced that I wanted to be a lighting designer and decided to find a college with a design program, the college advisers looked at me like I was crazy. I really didn't know anything about theater programs or colleges, but during my last year of high school, a children's theater group came to town. I worked with them and one of the crew told me about Carnegie Tech, which had a good theater program. I applied but didn't get in. It was the only school to which I had applied, and I had no idea what I was going to do.

"But one of the men who had directed a show at the community theater in which I worked was running the Berkshire Playhouse in Stockbridge, Massachusetts. He asked me to join them for the summer. I went and started as electrician/designer. When the summer was over, I came to New York and went to Lester Polakov's, where I took drafting courses and studied theater lighting. I started to work all over the city and did everything. I built scenery at the Cherry Lane Theatre and did odd jobs at off-off and off-Broadway theaters. I also worked in summer stock and did lighting for community theaters, which was very good practice.

"I also went to the theater all the time and watched load ins. I would just walk in and sit in the orchestra watching the sets and equipment brought in and set up onstage. That's how I got to know Tharon Musser [a prominent Tony Award–winning lighting designer]. When she was designing the lights for *Mame*, I sat there for four days from eight A.M. until midnight. She came over to me and said, 'I can't believe you've been here for so long,' and took me across the street for a drink. That summer, I went out of town to do more summer stock, and the next year I wrote her a letter asking if I could be her assistant. She hired me. That was in 1967 and I was twenty years old.

"The first projects I did with Tharon were five shows at the Stratford, Connecticut, Shakespeare Festival. Then I worked with her on the national company of *Mame*. All told, I worked on thirty-five shows during the five years I assisted Tharon. As an assistant, you do drafting, all the paperwork, write down the electric hook-ups, cue sheets, and focus charts. The designer creates and the assistant writes it all down. It's almost like being a secretary, except you are learning all about theater lighting.

"I left Tharon because I felt it was time to go out on my own, and my first show was the off-Broadway production of *Fortune and Men's Eyes*. Ken Waissman and Maxine Fox, who later produced *Grease*, were producing it as their first show. My first Broadway show was a Harold Prince production at the Ethel Barrymore Theatre, a revival of *The Visit*.

"I get involved at the very beginning of production. Sometimes, especially if it is a musical in development, there is not even a script yet when I meet with the director. We don't talk about specific lights, but we must make sure that we understand each other and are together in our concept of the show. We discuss color, mood, and the basic feel of the production. Usually, the set designer gets involved around the same time. Especially if the show is going to be a heavy lighting show, the set designer and I work together."

The set designer and the director collaborate in order to determine the basic style and/or approach for the show. Just as the set designer must create a stage setting that allows the actors to move and perform the movements set by the director, the set design must include room and positions for the lights.

"Those of us who work on the big musicals always work together. We discuss ideas and what we want to accomplish and do. I remember sitting down with Eugene Lee when he was doing sets for *Sweeney Todd* and I was doing the lights. It was very early in preproduction and he spoke about his idea of creating a huge foundry on stage. 'We can do a glass roof over it,' he said. And I said, 'Yes! But then we can get into foundry lighting. We'll have men with big searchlights, big hanging old foundry lamps, and the sun setting over the roof.' It just started coming and that's what showed up onstage. [One of the most dramatic moments in *Sweeney Todd* occurs when the glass roof of the foundry turns bloody red. It is the sun setting, but it is also symbolic of the events occurring onstage and an example of lighting augmenting and highlighting the dramatic action.] And while the set designer is working on the plans, we stay in touch. Many times, he'll call and say, 'I don't know how this is going to work. There's no place for the lights.' We'll get together and work it out. Often, his plans have to be revised on the basis of what my lighting needs will be.

"When the ground plans for the sets are complete, I can actually design the show. The one thing that is true about Broadway is that you are not limited by equipment. When you come into the theater, there is nothing there . . . just an empty space. We even have to bring in worklights. So all I am dealing with are the limitations of the actual stage space."

Lighting designers prepare a lighting plot. Comparable to a detailed map or blueprint, it indicates and identifies every single light that will be used for the production and specifies exactly where each will be placed. Some theaters have the pipes to which lights will be clamped, but often these must be ordered. The actual position of each pipe is numbered and indicated on the lighting plot, as are the colors that will be placed over the face of each light. These are called gels and are of a transparent polyester or mylar-coated material. Originally, gels were in fact gelatin formed into sheets. They must be cut to fit the frame of each light and are available in many colors and numbered according to color. The lighting designer prepares the lighting plot by placing tracing paper over the actual scaled ground plans for the set.

"I usually design all of my ideas and concepts into the plot.

Then, because of space and budget limitations, I pull back to what is the true essence of the design. I must also have leeway for when the director restages and makes major changes during rehearsals and previews.

"When the lighting plot is finished, I give it to the rental house from which all the lighting equipment for the production will be leased. All theatrical lighting equipment is rented [at least that is true for the Broadway commercial theater and its national, touring, and bus-and-truck companies]. When the lighting shop has a chance to look over my lighting plot, they call the general manager with a price and a deal is made. At that point, a production electrician is hired. I help choose the electrician, and his job is to make my plan a reality."

At the theater, special cable connects the lights to dimmers. The dimmers are situated in a dimmer rack that is located somewhere in the theater. Its position varies from theater to theater. In some it is backstage and in others it may be in the basement. Usually, each dimmer can handle 4,000 watts of electricity, so any number of lights with a combined wattage of 4,000 can be connected to a single dimmer. The dimmers are connected to a computer where the actual lighting cue information is stored.

The computer has revolutionized theatrical lighting. *A Chorus Line*, which opened in 1976, was the first time a computer was used on Broadway. Today, its use is routine. Prior to the advent of the computer, manually operated switchboards often took up much of the backstage area. Several electricians worked simultaneously, physically activating each lighting cue.

Today, the production electrician sits at the computer, operating the lights during the performance. Wearing a headset that is connected to one worn by the stage manager, he pushes the appropriate button on the computer, which corresponds to the cue being called. The computer sets up the previously programmed chain of events to successfully implement the cue.

Basically, a cue involves on/off, time, and intensity. The lighting activity generated by the cue can be a single on/off bump or last several minutes in duration. For instance, when the stage manager says, "Go light cue one," the electrician pushes the correct button on the computer's keyboard. The computer has been programmed for light cue one, which is, perhaps, a three-minute crossfade to the sunrise. For three minutes, lights of varying shades, intensities, and in various positions change, executing the cue.

At the electrical shop, the production electrician prepares the lights that have been ordered for the production. Organization is imperative here as the load in of all equipment into the theater normally takes place about a week before the first performance. Lights are usually the first heavy equipment installed, followed by the sets. Time at the theater is at a premium, and one of the tasks of the production electrician is to set up the lighting system so that it can be installed as quickly as possible the moment it is brought into the theater. The electrician makes sure that lighting pipes are properly labeled and that the exact positions for each light are indicated on the pipes. The cables that connect the lights with the dimmer racks are identified, and the gels that will be placed over each light are organized and numbered accordingly. Following the designer's lighting plot, the production electrician and house electricians work together, mounting the lights in correct position and height.

"When the lights are up, I go to the theater. I check to see if they've all been hung correctly, and then we focus the lights. This means aiming the lights to get them focused onto the correct places. I stand on the stage and the electrician climbs a ladder and puts each light on. We make sure that it is where it should be and then I'll say, 'Okay, lock it' and he takes his wrenches and locks all the nuts and bolts, securing the light to the lighting pipe. We do this for each light. There can be over five hundred lights and it often involves two ten-hour days.

"Don't forget that the electrician doesn't know what the lights are supposed to do. He's hung them where I've indicated they should be placed. But he has no idea that one of the lights will act as a special spot on an actress when she sings her big song from the top of the stairs, or that we will be showing a descent into a dungeon. I've been going to rehearsals and know how the director is staging the show. The light focus is based upon the information I have from collaborating with the director and actually seeing him work. I do, however, leave some spare equipment for ways to get myself out of trouble, because it is inevitable that changes will be made and the staging will be different once the show gets onstage. My job is always to say, 'I can do it' when the director asks me if a change can be made. That's why I've been hired. Even if the lights are hung and focused, I must leave myself a margin of safety so that I can do what the director wants.

"When the sound equipment, scenery, and lights are installed, the actors and director come into the theater and we begin tech. That's when I actually start doing the cueing. This is the point where I am creating the stage picture. Understanding basic electricity, how lights work, how they should be hung, and how to program the computer are only the tools for me to work with. This is where the art begins."

The tech rehearsal is the time during which the acting and

technical elements of the production are fused. As the actors go through the performance, Billington creates the lighting that will accompany and highlight their stage actions and movements.

"I sit in the middle of the theater wearing a headset connected to the production electrician, who is sitting at the computer console. As the actors rehearse, I tell the electrician which lights to turn on and at what intensity. As the cues are finalized, my assistant notes them. Basically, I light the show during tech, fix it during dress rehearsal, and polish and make it work during previews.

"The thing about the theater is that you just never have enough time. More frequently than not, I have to refocus the lights and change cues, but there just isn't time for me to have time alone onstage just to work with the lights. Everybody knows I need it, but the director is usually using every bit of rehearsal time for restaging and polishing. The scenery is being adjusted and fixed and the lighting time becomes less and less. Finally, I say that at some point I must have some hours to clean up the lighting. I usually get it after we've been in preview for a while and only because there's a reason the cast can't be onstage. For instance, I might get my stage time only because there's an Equity meeting which everyone is attending. Usually, if I get four hours alone, I'm lucky.

"But the thing to remember is that here we are in a Broadway theater, with the most famous creative people, putting on a big, original musical. We have stars and are spending millions of dollars. The stakes are tremendous! You simply cannot go any further in the musical theater. This is it! So my goal is to have the lights finished and polished by opening night. I can't stand there and scream and stomp my feet because I'm not getting the time I need. If I did, I'd never have the opportunity to do this again. No one is going to deal with a prima donna lighting designer. But when all the elements come together and an audience has one of those rare and incredible experiences in the theater, then you know you've done it. It doesn't happen often, but when it does, it's magical."

Sound Design

One of the most recent theatrical design specialties is sound. Only in the last ten years has the credit "sound designed by" appeared on billing sheets and in programs. It is a small profession, limited mostly to the commercial theater. Regionally and off-Broadway, sound usually involves sound effects rather than reinforcement, which involves putting microphones on performers and instruments to improve their audibility and clarity throughout the theater. The cost of sound equipment is prohibitive, and most small theaters do not present shows that require amplification and sophisticated audio installations.

The emergence of the sound designer is a logical consequence to changes in the acting profession, audience tastes, and technology. Today, actors routinely move back and forth between heavily miked television and movie studios, and the theater. Many are not trained to project their voices and require vocal reinforcement when working before live audiences.

At the same time, many of today's audiences are used to record orchestrations. They tend to be lush and heavy, and since the 1950s, more often than not, loud and rock-inspired. Whereas music for the theater used to be scored to support the vocal line, today's musical orchestrations reflect these changing tastes and are often scored more for recordings. Audiences can't hear vocal lines over certain instruments. Yet electric guitars, synthesizers, and other amplified instruments are commonly used in most musical entertainments. Microphones, particularly wireless mikes that can be attached to performers allowing for free movement onstage, have made it possible to amplify voices to compensate for this. This is easier said than done, and increasingly theater sound is under attack by both critics and theatergoers as it gets louder and the vocal and instrumental balance becomes increasingly harsh and abrasive to the ear.

Otts Munderloh is a sound designer who has designed the sound for the Broadway shows *Barnum, Ballroom, I Remember Mama, Ain't Misbehavin', Sophisticated Ladies,* and the 1982 musical hit *Dreamgirls.*

*   *   *

"I went to Marlboro College in Vermont, where I majored in drama and minored in organic chemistry. I had always planned to be in the theater, but didn't really know what I would do. In 1969 I took a semester off from college and was in Baltimore, where we were living, when a family friend who was David Merrick's production electrician asked me if I would like to run the sound for the bus-and-truck company of *I Do, I Do.* I told him that I knew nothing about sound, but he said, 'Be in Wilmington on September 4.' So I went. For ten months I did one-nighters all over the country. It was a terrific experience. When the tour was over, I went back to school and then was asked to do the bus and truck of *Company.*

"After that, I hung around Baltimore for a couple of years and did some work in Washington, D.C. Then the soundman

who had taught me everything on *I Do, I Do* asked me to
come to New York to take over the sound on *Ulysses in Night-
town*. There I met Abe Jacob, my mentor [Jacob is one of the
most respected sound designers in the theater and one of the
first to specialize in theatrical sound], and started to work for
him. I ran the sound on *Seesaw* with Lucie Arnaz, *A Little
Night Music, Chicago*, and *Mack and Mabel*. I had joined the
union in this really nefarious way by going to Scranton, Pennsylvania, which is where I am originally from, and joining the
Scranton local.

"It was around that time that I met Michael Bennett
[creator of *A Chorus Line* and *Dreamgirls*]. He kept saying,
'I'm doing a show with dancers and I'm going to do it on a
bare stage' and I kept telling him that I was really busy and
couldn't work for him. I had a lot of shows to do for Abe and
was about to go out of town with *Chicago*. When I came back
to New York, I went to see Michael's show, which turned out
to be *A Chorus Line*. It wasn't on Broadway yet and when I
saw it, I said to myself, 'I made the wrong decision.'

"But one day, while I was in the middle of running *Chicago*, I turned around and there were Michael and Abe.
Michael had decided to fire the soundman on *A Chorus Line*,
which was previewing on Broadway and about to open. Abe
had designed the sound and I was asked to run it. So I moved
to *Chorus Line* and opened the show. Then Abe and I split
tours of *Chorus Line*, and at that point I started doing shows
on my own as a sound designer."

Munderloh believes that most Broadway shows are over-
amplified. The crux of the problem, he feels, lies neither with
the sound designer nor sound system, but stems from unreal
expectations on the part of the producer or director.

"You have to rely on taste and judgment. There's nothing

you can write down for sound because it's all subjective. That's the trouble with it. You can take meter readings and follow them for each show, but if you're watching meters, then you're not really doing your job, which is listening. It's not about the equipment. It's about personalities, orchestrations, and directors.

"Usually, when a show is in trouble and the producer or director start getting nervous, the sound level gets turned up. It all depends upon who has the power. As you go and work in this business, you realize that there are very few people who will really let you do your job well.

"The other problem is orchestrations. People are used to hearing record orchestrations, but you really can't do that in the theater. If you cover a voice, you can't hear it. That's always been true. When you start putting instruments under the voice, it gets difficult. On a record you can have a thick, heavy orchestration, which is what people are used to hearing today. You can't do that in the theater, but no one wants to know that. With the advent of the microphone, people think that it means you can now put record orchestrations onstage.

"In *Dreamgirls* I have wireless mikes on people and, sometimes, when the orchestra gets too loud, I can make the mikes louder, but sometimes I can't. It really depends upon the orchestrations. Sometimes they're so loud that I know I'm going to have to amplify the singers. But the problem is that, in the theater, the vocal level has to be a proportional amount louder than the orchestra or else the audience just can't hear the vocal."

Originally, the sound designer was supposed to make it possible for those sitting in the rear of the theater to hear as well as those in the front.

"Somehow, we've gone from filling in Row U to Row A. I

always think that if you can't hear the sound from the stage without amplification in the first ten rows, you're in trouble. You either have the wrong people singing onstage or the wrong orchestrations. You just can't have record orchestrations in the theater and hear sound from the stage. If you do that, you have to put a wireless microphone on the performer and the voice will come out of a speaker. And that's when you end up hearing a loud orchestra from the pit and a voice from the speaker. Whenever you start putting instruments under the voice, it gets difficult. People think that today, because of technology—foot mikes, wireless mikes—you can do anything. But it's not true, and what works in a recording studio won't work onstage. *Oklahoma* had no mikes and I'm sure the audience heard every word."

Sound is not only a relatively new specialty, but it is also not easily understood. Before there were sound designers, electricians handled basic sound equipment, which usually included some foot mikes, an amplifier, and two speakers. Today, sound design is part of all Broadway musicals and involves thousands of dollars worth of equipment. Sound equipment is rented, with the production usually paying a weekly rental of one percent of the equipment's value. *Dreamgirls* has $400,000 worth of equipment.

Loudspeakers are hung in clusters or individually throughout the theater. Monitors mounted onstage allow the performers to hear the orchestra, since the stage overhangs the orchestra pit, propelling the instrumental sound forward into the theater and away from the stage area. Foot mikes and offstage vocal booths in which singers can supplement chorus numbers or perform without being seen are routine to sound design. Wireless mikes are attached to performers and individual instruments are miked. All of these are connected to a console from which the actual sound is mixed or regulated during the performance.

The sound designer visits the theater well in advance of production to ascertain its sound capabilities both in terms of acoustics and equipment. Once this is done and the needs of the production determined, the sound designer arranges to rent and install the equipment. However, it is only when the orchestra and cast are onstage together that the designer can really begin to ascertain and effect the quality of the production's sound.

"You get involved early in the production, but no one pays attention. You mark the stage to indicate where the microphones will be placed, but most directors won't plan any staging around them. You try to put the mikes so that wherever the actors stop onstage, they're in the right position, but sometimes the director has to bend. You have to plead or cajole. A lot of it depends upon how much trust I have from the director. For instance, in *Chorus Line*, there is a moment where the character of Sheila comes downstage and starts to sing. Well, initially when she moved, she wasn't at the mike. Michael revised the staging. Now, every Sheila in every company of *Chorus Line* goes downstage and then takes a few steps across. That's not a directorial necessity, but it is a sound necessity. But a lot of directors aren't like Michael. They expect sound to accomplish everything. They think that they've had the actors in rehearsal for six weeks and that all the technical stuff can be accomplished onstage within two days. But it just doesn't work that way.

"When we were doing *Dreamgirls* in Boston before coming to Broadway, we had to cancel two previews. I had gone to the conductor, the composer, and the orchestrator and kept saying that the music was just too loud. They kept saying that it would be okay when the band was in the pit. Well, we got into the theater and played the first number and Michael said, 'I have no show! I can't hear a thing!' We all went out to dinner and discussed what we could do. We decided to put the rhythm section in a Plexiglas booth for the Boston run.

"There was also a saxophone line right under the vocal line and, of course, the audience couldn't hear the vocal. Michael said, 'What are we going to do about that?' And I said, 'Cut it out.' Well, Michael said, 'But I want a musical here.' As it turned out, it was cut. But people get confused and scared the closer you get to opening night. They begin to think that the louder everything is, the better and they just will not understand the basic dynamic between vocal and orchestra."

Unlike sets, costumes, and lights, which are completed by opening and subsequently placed, worn, or operated according to precisely indicated cues, sound design is an ongoing process. The sound designer can select the best possible equipment, deciding how it shall be used to enhance the production. But good sound involves a lot more than reacting to prearranged cues and implementing a designer's plan.

A sound operator mixes the sound at each performance. He is influenced by what is happening onstage, in the orchestra pit, and in the audience. Most designers either run their own shows during performance or choose someone with whom they routinely work.

It takes two people to run the sound for *Dreamgirls*. The sound team sits at the rear of the theater's orchestra section, facing a huge console with inputs connected to each monitor, speaker, and microphone used during the show. There are microphones attached to each section of the orchestra. For instance, there are two mikes for the four trumpets, a separate mike for each reed instrument, and six mikes for the percussion section. Foot mikes onstage are wired into this console, as are each of the wireless mikes worn by the performers. Phones connect with the backstage area and the musical director.

The sound operators constantly adjust tone and volume. One works the vocals and the other works the orchestra. Much of this is subjective, determined by the audience and the needs of the actor. If an audience is particularly up and excited, the sound level will be kept louder throughout the show. If one of the singers is having an off night or misses a position near a foot mike during a solo number, the vocal volume will be turned up. Certain instruments must be accented in some songs and diminished in others.

In addition, many problems can occur with so much technical equipment. Even though prerecorded cassettes are used during parts of the show for special sound effects—for instance, an offstage announcer or a recording—the musical director must be able to keep the orchestra playing in time and on cue. In order to do this he wears a headset through which a steady beat gives a count, indicating the tempo for the orchestra and the point at which the next cue must be given to a singer. If this headset malfunctions, the entire show can be thrown off. In addition, wireless mikes often malfunction and intricate technical equipment breaks down, causing a change in pace and quality that might not be immediately discernible to the audience but can, in fact, change the show. The sound operators make repairs and substitutions during the performance.

Munderloh has a team of four people who work on the shows he designs. Currently running the sound on *Dreamgirls* himself, he feels that "real sound" is the goal in the theater and what he tries to achieve.

"The real trick is sitting in the theater and making it all work. It's not the equipment. So much of it is subjective.

Basically, good sound comes from people. If the musical director can't hear the singers, he should bring down the orchestra. The vocal level must be a proportional amount louder than the orchestra or else the audience won't hear it. If the orchestra is turned up ten points, the vocal has to go up twenty. On a record, you can decrease that margin and still hear the vocal clearly. But you can't do that in the theater. With sound, less is more."

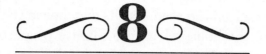

At the Theater— Production Jobs

There are many people whose work in the theater is literally "behind the scenes." The artistic people have the responsibility to open the show. They then go on to other projects, sometimes returning if there is a major cast change or the show begins to tour and must be redesigned. Others continue to work at the theater, running and maintaining the production and the theater in which it plays.

The Crew

The crew is made up of the stagehands who set up the stage, move the scenery, and run the lights and sound during each performance. In the commercial theater, a crew member must be a member of the International Alliance of Theatrical Stage Employees (IATSE).

Crew members are hired either by the production company to work specifically for the show or by the theater to oversee its maintenance as well as to work on the show. These workers are hired as part of the carpentry, lighting, property, or sound crew. Each area has carefully defined and distinct responsibilities.

Each theater that houses commercial productions, either in New York or on the road, has its own house staff. Heading the staff are the house electrician, house propertyman, and house carpenter. They are hired by the theater under a contract that goes from Labor Day to Labor Day. They do not work, however, if the house is dark. When there is a show in the theater, they go on payroll.

Each production hires its own propertyman, carpenter, and electrician. They are specialists who work for the production company. Production personnel hold "pink contracts" or "road contracts" and house personnel hold "white contracts." Those holding pink contracts are permitted to work for the production in a city in which they are not members of the IATSE local, although they must be IATSE members. Those holding white contracts must be members of the IATSE local that has jurisdiction over the town in which they are working.

The house department heads hire the crew members who work in the theater and on the show. Called casuals, they work by the hour, the day, or by the performance. A regular salary scale is set on the basis of eight performances a week. In New York, the house crew members belong to Local 1, the most powerful and influential of the IATSE stagehand locals and the most difficult to gain admission to.

Long holding a reputation as a "father/son" union, IATSE admission requirements vary from local to local. For Local 1, however, the basic requirement for membership is the successful completion of a general-knowledge examination after which you are placed on a waiting list until an apprentice position becomes available. You must then accumulate a certain amount of work experience each year for three years, after which you are placed on an admissions list. Each month, five names are drawn out of a hat and those lucky enough to have their names drawn become members.

Many people, particularly those who work under pink contracts, join IATSE through a local other than Local 1. Out of town, there are residency requirements, and the fact remains that for stagehands, IATSE is not an easy union to get into under any circumstances. But sometimes, depending upon the local and your particular circumstances, the membership process can be simplified.

Production Propertyman

Hired by and under contract to the production company, the production propertyman works with the stage manager, designers, director, and actors in purchasing, gathering, setting up, and even making all the properties that are used in the production.

Jan Marasek is a production propertyman. He has worked for most of the producers active in the commercial theater both in New York and on the road.

* * *

"I started out as an actor, but I always seemed to have some natural technical skill. I did a lot of off-Broadway and helped with electrical work. I gradually got into production and was lighting designer for José Quintero when he was just starting Circle in the Square.

"Over the years, I was in and out of theater. I did underwater photography for a while and traveled around the world. When I did decide to stay in the theater, I spent about six years doing summer stock, winter stock—you name it—all kinds of theater before I did Broadway. I got into the union in 1955. I had been sponsored by another propertyman, but I still had to wait three years to become a member. It was easier to get in then than it is now. My first Broadway show was *A Hole in the Head* at the Martin Beck Theatre, where I was an assistant to the production propertyman.

"I work for the production, which means that someone, usually the general manager, calls and asks me if I'm interested in doing a show. I find out the schedule, whether it's going to go out of town or not, and what kind of show it is. If it's a very heavy show, I hire an assistant to work with me. I've learned that you have to ask for things that you know you're going to need.

"I remember the most difficult show I ever did was Neil Simon's *The Good Doctor*. And it wasn't even that it was such a heavy show. It was just that I hadn't asked for help and was just doing too much. I was working with Tony Walton who wanted a lot of realism and insisted that every detail be exact. Usually, you can't spend too much money on props and I have to improvise . . . even in a big expensive musical. On this show, though, I was running all over town trying to get hold of fourteen real gold watches and countless other things. I had no staff. We got the show going but I never stopped working.

"I usually know I'm going to be working on a show about a month in advance. Sometimes though, I don't go on contract until a week before the show is onstage. It all depends. Years ago, when shows actually used to rehearse in the theater itself, a propertyman was hired right away. Today, shows rehearse in studios and they're always trying to save money. So I don't sign a contract until it's crucial that I start getting things together.

"When I start work, the first thing I do is call up the designers and find out what they're going to want. The stage manager also gives me a list of props. Sometimes, I'm asked to get rehearsal props. Usually though, the stage manager gets someone else to do it or does it himself. Rehearsal props are different from the props used onstage. You're not supposed to use the same ones.

"Once I find out what is going to be needed, I start getting everything together. I've got to please the designers, the director, and the actors. For instance, if the designer wants books, I usually buy old books by the foot. Sometimes, there has to be a certain look to the books. If it seems like it's going to get complicated and I have time, I photograph the books before buying them and show the photo to the designer and director. The designer might like them, but the director may say, 'No, I want them to look thicker' or 'I want them to look like medical books,' which have a different look to them. Sometimes, I even have to tone down the color of a book so that it blends in with the scenery in a certain way.

"If there's food, I like to make it myself. If the actor actually eats onstage, I make sure that the real food is there, on cue, for each performance. But if there's time to make the platters of food or fruit that might appear onstage, I do. I once made a whole turkey that could be cut up so that the bones and carcass showed. Even food has to be exacting. When I was doing *The Good Doctor*, the director hated the color green. I couldn't have any green books onstage and I even had to spray the celery I made so that it wouldn't appear so green.

"I make plaster casts if they're needed. It's a time-consuming job, because unlike a real cast, which dries on the person and remains in place until it's time to take it off, the actor must be able to remove it and it must be precisely fitted. You can't forget that the actor must be comfortable using the props. Sometimes an actor will come to me and say that the position of a prop—like a telephone which he has to hold—is uncomfortable. I have to do something about it, but I also have to be sure that whatever I do doesn't interfere with specific stage directions. In this job, you have to please everybody.

"I'm responsible for liquor which is drunk onstage. Of course, I don't use real liquor, but I've had some shows where the actor will ask me to substitute real liquor for what I use. I can't take on that kind of responsibility, of course. I have to go to the stage manager and ask him.

"I get pillows, rugs, lamps—you name it. I have a lot of sources, which I've discovered over the years. I never stop looking, even if I'm not working or searching for something specific. Usually, even if I see something that I know I'll probably never need, I can get an idea for another prop or how to make something.

"Basically, I work on the street. If I'm setting up a show, that's where I am most of the time. I'm always on the move, going from place to place, picking up things and looking for other things. The rule is: If you can't buy it, you make it."

In the commercial theater, electricians, carpenters, and propertymen have separate and distinct responsibilities. Although most IATSE locals have contracts that detail similar responsibilities and divisions of labor, certain prop responsibilities in one city can be carpentry responsibilities in another and vice versa.

"On the set, everything except a wall and the floor is usually a prop. Linoleum, rugs, and other floor coverings are props. If there's a kitchen onstage, I get the appliances and install them, except if there's a sink with running water. I install it, but the electrician is responsible for it because water is part of his responsibility. If there is a lamp which is connected to live current on the stage, I buy it and place it in position. But the electrician plugs it in. Any problem with doors or windows are part of carpentry. Shades and curtains are mine, although hanging draperies are usually carpentry. If a major repair job on part of the set is needed and it is 'artistic work,' a scenic artist comes in to touch it up. I'll do stain work and I'm permitted to do a straight color. These are just things you learn over the years. If there are ever problems about who does what, an arbitrator comes in. But that hardly ever happens."

The production propertyman tours with the show if it goes on the road. He is responsible for duplicating the traveling show so that it is identical to the original production (except when the designer has made changes and adjustments for the traveling show).

"When the show tours, my job is to make it identical in each place. Before we take down the set in New York, I photograph it so I know exactly what it looks like and which objects go where. I also mark each prop and put special hardware on things that will be mounted, so that they will be more secure. We used to do that before the show opened on Broadway, but now we wait until we know whether the show is going to run or not. Nobody wants to spend money before he has to."

If the show remains in New York and national companies are formed, the production propertyman must duplicate the props for each company. In the few instances when a show is such a hit as to have a Broadway production and several national and touring companies, the production propertyman often sets up the show in each city, leaving an assistant to assume the day-to-day responsibility for running the show and working with the local crew.

"Basically, my job is to execute the design and to make it

practical for the actor. It requires a lot of experience. My rule of thumb is that you have to work on at least five shows before you can even get a feel for what has to be done. You never stop learning."

House Propertyman
The house propertyman is employed by the theater. He works with the production propertyman running the show's props, but is also responsible for those tasks in the theater that come under his jurisdiction. He repairs, installs, or maintains the theater's seats, mirrors in the dressing room, and lavatories and most of the theater's nonelectric movable fixtures and furniture.

Property Master/Propertyman
In the not-for-profit theater, this position is nonunion and resembles more the work of the production propertyman than house propertyman. The theater's maintenance staff usually handles repairs within the body of the theater. A multitheater complex usually employs a property master who works with the designers and obtains and executes the props used for a show. When there are several shows in production at one time, a staff of propertymen work under the direction of the property master, each running a show and responsible for the maintenance of that show's props.

Production Electrician
The production electrician works with the lighting designer and executes the lighting plan conceived by the designer. He decides how many people will be needed to run the lights for a production, maintains all electrical equipment, operates the switchboard or computer for lighting cues, and arranges and focuses all lighting instruments.

House Electrician
The house electrician works with the production electrician but also maintains the theater's lighting fixtures, chandeliers, and all other electrical equipment (with the exception of really heavy equipment that is handled by the engineer). Anything that involves water comes under the domain of the house electrician. He supervises the house crew of lighting operators and is responsible for turning on and off the house-lights.

Electrician
This is a nonunion job in not-for-profit theater. The electrician parallels the job of production and house electrician. In some theaters, the electrician functions as lighting designer on some or all productions.

Production Carpenter
The production carpenter works with the set designer and makes sure that the sets are properly installed at the theater and the equipment maintained and repaired during the run of the show. Sometimes, if a set is particularly elaborate, the production carpenter works while the set is actually being built at the scenic shop. Increasingly, as sets become technologically more elaborate, a technical supervisor is hired to work during the period of the load in to help smooth out the problems that will inevitably arise with winches, turntables, and other complicated equipment.

House Carpenter
The house carpenter supervises the house crew and hires the crew that will work on the production. Under his domain comes the rigger, who installs equipment that raises or lowers scenery, and the flyer, who raises and lowers scenery

from storage to stage areas and raises and lowers the curtain. In addition, the house carpenter maintains those areas of the theater that come under his jurisdiction including doors, windows, and the actual stage.

Carpenter

In not-for-profit theater, the carpenter often has added responsibilities. If the theater has its own scenery building shop, the staff carpenter often builds the scenery or adapts scenery from past productions to make it usable for another production.

Wardrobe

Wardrobe Supervisor

In the commercial theater, the wardrobe supervisor is in charge of all costumes. He makes sure that they are in good repair and clean. He is responsible for all the costume changes that must be made during the performance and supervises a staff of dressers who work with individual performers.

In the not-for-profit theater, the equivalent position is costumier. Often the costumier designs costumes for productions when an outside designer isn't retained. Ordinarily, however, the costumier supervises the costume shop where costumes are constructed, stored, and maintained. He has charge of executing costume designs and functions as wardrobe supervisor with the same tasks as his commercial counterpart.

In the commercial theater, the wardrobe supervisor is a member of the Wardrobe Supervisors and Dressers Union (WSDU). A potential member must be a resident of whatever city or state over which the union local has jurisdiction for a minimum of eighteen months and must be sponsored by a union member. Only about ten to twenty new members are accepted each year by Local 764, which is the New York City local. When the production travels, the wardrobe supervisor travels with the show but hires members of the city's local as dressers.

Dresser

The dresser is responsible for getting a particular performer onstage, at the right time and in the right costume. He maintains the costume over which he has responsibility. Dressers are also members of the union, although there are two exceptions. An actor with star billing (meaning that the actor's name appears above the title of the play) may choose his own dresser whether the dresser is union or nonunion. In addition, if the union doesn't have enough dressers available who are able to work on a particular show, nonunion dressers selected from the union's membership waiting list may be hired.

Stephanie Edwards is a Broadway wardrobe supervisor.

* * *

"I started as a dancer. I went to UCLA as a dance major, but it is difficult to support yourself as a dancer. I worked in New York and all around the country and organized my own dance company in Los Angeles. I wasn't making much money and I also realized I was getting older and had probably gone as far as I would as a dancer. So I decided that the time had come to look for something else.

"I had married an actor and moved to New York. He was about to open in a new show, *On Golden Pond.* I had always known how to sew, and he introduced me to Frances Sternhagen, who was starring in the Broadway production and needed a dresser. I became her dresser for the show, and when it closed a friend recommended me to Sandy Duncan who was starring in *Peter Pan*. From *Peter Pan* I went to work as an assistant wardrobe supervisor for *Onward Victoria* and then on to *Woman of the Year* starring Lauren Bacall, Hal Prince's *Merrily We Roll Along*, and as wardrobe supervisor for the revival of Neil Simon's musical, *Little Me*.

"As wardrobe supervisor, all the costumes become my responsibility from the moment they leave the costume shop. As soon as I am hired for the production, I read the script and do a rough costume plot. This lists every costume and accessory worn by each performer and indicates when they are worn in the performance. I must know exactly when each costume change must come and how much time each change will require. The kind of backstage organization and setup will depend upon that information.

"Basically, I work out all the systems. I decide whether we will need quick-change booths in the wings, or if actors will have time to go back to their dressing rooms to change. I work out precise systems that the dressers will use in bringing the new costumes to the actors and taking the worn ones away. I even work out motions that will be used while performing costume changes so that there will be minimal disturbance to hair and makeup. I also determine the number of dressers we will need. Stars have their own dressers and some other actors do as well [this is determined after negotiation and is part of an actor's contract], but the number of dressers we hire depends upon the number of costumes there are in the show, how complicated the changes are, and how quickly they must be done.

"This is often a physically exhausting job. In *Little Me* we had a lot of trouble keeping dressers. We were in a theater with very little backstage space. It's a period musical with a lot of very big, heavy, and elaborate costumes. We also had actors who had to leave the stage, make a change, and almost immediately appear again onstage. The changes had to be made in the wings and there was no room to store any of the costumes. The dressers had to run up and down the stairs throughout the performance, carrying these heavy costumes. It amounted to about two and a half hours of intense physical work for each performance. A lot of the dressers who usually work Broadway shows just couldn't handle it.

"After the show opens, I am responsible for maintaining and replacing the costumes. Most costumes are made like very fine clothing. The designer's responsibility is over on opening night, but the costumes require constant attention. We can do some of the work at the theater, but often we have to send the costumes out to a seamstress for major repairs.

"The whole business of wardrobe has changed. Dressers used to be the wives of stagehands, but today most of the dressers are younger. Many thought that they wanted to be designers and then just decided that designing was too much. Designers tend to be in production all the time, which is totally time-consuming. For a dresser, if things work out, you can have a job for the run of the show and don't have to work all day.

"Most of what I do involves dealing with people. It's a good idea to know how to sew and know how the costumes are constructed. But I am always dealing with staff and actors and I'm often in the position of solving problems that occur between my staff and actors. Costumes are very important to actors. They are one of the tangible pieces of the show. So, in addition to being an effective administrator, a wardrobe supervisor must be good at dealing with people."

Appendix

Organizations and Associations

Many organizations offer internship and training programs and employment placement services for aspiring theater professionals. In addition, many of the nation's not-for-profit regional theaters offer seasonal and/or summer internship opportunities. For a listing of these theaters, the best source is *Theatre Profiles*, which is published by the Theatre Communications Group (see listing under publications).

> The Alliance of Resident Theatres/New York
> 353 Spring Street
> New York, New York 10013
> (212) 989-5257

ART/New York is an organization composed of more than eighty of New York City's not-for-profit professional theaters. It provides its members with services and information in the areas of management training, audience development, public relations, and funding, and oversees two internship programs.

Theatre Management Internship/New York is a formal internship program in which graduate and undergraduate students are placed for a minimum of one semester with one of the Alliance's participating theaters or arts institutions. These are management and production internships. Students participate in a comprehensive fifteen-week seminar series in which leading New York theater professionals discuss a broad range of topics relevant to both the not-for-profit and commercial theater.

Direct Line is an ongoing, informal program that places students and volunteers with member theaters according to the needs and interests of each. Placements can be for a single production or an entire semester.

Alternate ROOTS
c/o Nexus
360 Fortune Street, NE
Atlanta, Georgia 30312
(404) 577-1079

Alternate ROOTS (Regional Organization for Theatres South) serves as a clearinghouse for the exchange of work and information among southern performing artists and arts organizations.

American Council on the Arts
570 Seventh Avenue
New York, New York 10018
(212) 354-6655

American Council on the Arts is a national arts service organization that promotes and strengthens cultural activities in the United States. Through its extensive body of publications, it provides information on all aspects of arts management and offers seminars and training sessions on policies affecting the arts.

American Theatre Association
1000 Vermont Avenue, NW
Washington, D.C. 20005
(202) 628-4634

The American Theatre Association is dedicated to the development of noncommercial theater. Its five constituent organizations include the American Community Theatre Association, University College Theatre Association, Secondary School Theatre Association, Children's Theatre Association, and Army Theatre Arts Association. An annual convention offers a variety of workshops and seminars dealing with the arts and there are regional and statewide conferences organized by the constituent organizations throughout the year.

California Theatre Council
6253 Hollywood Blvd.
Los Angeles, California 90028
(213) 465-6153

CTC is an information clearinghouse for more than one hundred not-for-profit professional theaters in California. It organizes an annual state-wide conference and seminars in management and administration.

Foundation for the Extension and Development
  of the American Professional Theatre (FEDAPT)
165 West 46th Street
New York, New York 10036
(212) 869-9690

FEDAPT is a national not-for-profit service organization that helps development, administrative, and management capabilities of theater and dance groups throughout the United States. FEDAPT holds a three-day national conference in New York City on theater management and offers consultation services on box office management, boards of trustees, theater management, and technical assistance.

The Great Lakes Colleges Association
  New York Arts Program
308 West 48th Street
New York, New York 10036
(212) 582-9088

The Great Lakes Colleges Association is a consortium of twelve colleges in the Midwest. The New York Arts Program is open to students from all accredited institutions and places them in apprenticeships in New York City arts organizations. Students receive training and college credit and participate in a series of seminars conducted by representatives from various areas of the arts.

National Endowment for the Arts
2401 E Street, NW
Washington, D.C. 20506
(202) 634-6387—theater
(202) 634-6586—fellowship program

The National Endowment for the Arts is a federal agency created in 1965 by an act of Congress to promote and support the arts in the United States. Through grants, the NEA supports many arts organizations.

Its National Endowment Fellowship Program for Arts Managers brings arts administrators to the NEA offices in Washington for thirteen-week periods. Applicants usually have had professional experience in some phase of arts management or hold an advanced degree. Fellows work as members of the NEA staff and have the opportunity to learn about policy development, grant-making procedures, and administration.

Opportunity Resources for the Arts
1501 Broadway
New York, New York 10036
(212) 575-1688

Opportunities Resources is a not-for-profit national placement agency that serves arts centers, arts councils, performing arts organizations, museums, historical organizations, science centers, visual arts organizations, and arts service organizations, and individuals seeking employment in the arts. It provides personnel information, counseling, and placement services.

Performing Arts Management Institution (PAMI)
408 West 57th Street
New York, New York 10019
(212) 245-3850

PAMI sponsors a yearly three-day course that is designed to supplement the knowledge and skills of professionals and students interested in managing cultural institutions.

Theatre Communications Group, Inc. (TCG)
355 Lexington Avenue
New York, New York 10017

TCG is the national service organization for the not-for-profit professional theater in the United States. Its membership is composed of more than two hundred constituent and associate theaters as well as thousands of individuals. It offers member theaters assistance in casting, professional recruitment, and development, including management, fundraising, and literary services. TCG's extensive publications include: *Theatre Profiles*, a biennial guide to not-for-profit theaters; *Theatre Communications*, a monthly publication containing features and articles pertaining to the not-for-profit theater; *Dramatists Sourcebook*; and *ArtSEARCH*, a listing of job opportunities in the performing arts that is published every two weeks.

Unions

In order to work in the commercial theater, you will most likely have to join a union. It is not easy to gain admittance to theatrical unions. When you do join a union, in many cases you join a local that is a branch of the union. Often you can work only in the geographical area over which the particular local has jurisdiction. The following is a list of the major theatrical unions. For information and admissions procedures, contact the national office of the union or the local you wish to join.

American Federation of Musicians
1500 Broadway
New York, New York 10036
(212) 869-1330

This union represents musicians, arrangers, copyists, orchestrators, librarians, and proofreaders. There are 604 locals throughout the United States and Canada.

Association of Theatrical Press Agents
    and Managers (ATPAM)
165 West 46th Street
New York, New York 10036
(212) 719-3666

This is the union for company managers, house managers, and press agents who work in the legitimate theater throughout the United States and Canada. There are two apprenticeship programs for aspiring members: the press agent apprenticeship program is administered by ATPAM and the manager apprenticeship program is jointly administered by AT-PAM and the League of New York Theatres and Producers.

Press agent apprentices must be under contract to a senior press agent and complete sixty weeks' working credit in three years. Only five press agent apprentices are accepted each year and in addition to the work requirements they must pass an examination and complete a series of seminars for admittance to ATPAM.

Managers must be sponsored by a general manager and must complete fifty weeks of credited employment within two years. The number accepted as apprentices varies each year, but all accepted apprentices must complete a series of seminars and successfully pass an examination before acceptance into ATPAM.

The International Alliance of
  Theatrical Stage Employees (IATSE)
1515 Broadway (National Office)
New York, New York 10036
(212) 730-1770

This is the largest of the theatrical unions and represents personnel in both theater and film. There are more than nine hundred locals representing different professional categories, and each has a different admissions policy.

Local 1—represents stage carpenters, propertymen, and
  electricians
1775 Broadway
New York, New York 10019
(212) 489-7710

Local 764—represents theatrical wardrobe attendants
1501 Broadway
New York, New York 10036
(212) 221-1717

Local 751—represents treasurers and ticket sellers
227 West 45th Street
New York, New York 10036
(212) 489-7710

Society of Stage Directors and
  Choreographers (SSDC)
1501 Broadway
New York, New York 10036
(212) 391-1070

The Society of Stage Directors and Choreographers (SSDC) is an independent national labor union that represents directors and choreographers in all sectors of the legitimate theater.

United Scenic Artists (USA), Local 829
1540 Broadway
New York, New York 10036
(212) 575-5120

United Scenic Artists (USA), Local 350
343 South Dearborn Street
Chicago, Illinois 60604
(312) 431-0790

USA Local 829 is an autonomous local of the Brotherhood of Painters and Allied Trades. The only other local affiliated with the brotherhood is Local 350 in Chicago. USA has jurisdiction over scenic designers, costume designers, and lighting designers. Entrance is determined by the completion of an exam that consists of an interview, a home project, and a practical that tests the applicant's skills under pressure of severe time limitation.

Schools

In the last twenty years, colleges and universities have begun to offer degrees in arts administration and management. Most schools offer undergraduate courses in theater arts including directing, acting, and design. Many undergraduate institutions offer courses in management and administration as well. Below are listed those schools that offer graduate degrees in arts administration and management. The programs vary, some offering business administration and arts management and others more specifically theater-oriented. For more information, you can consult the American Theatre Association's *Directory of American College Theatre* or *A Survey of Arts Administration Training in the United States and Canada,* which is available through the American Council for the Arts (see organization and association listing for addresses of ATA and ACA). In addition, *Theatre Crafts* often contains information on both undergraduate and graduate programs through both advertising and editorial information.

Adelphi University
Garden City, New York 11530
(516) 294-8700

Program: Graduate Certificate in Management of the Arts, School of Business Administration.

The American University
Washington, D.C. 20016
(202) 686-2314

Program: Master of Arts in Arts Administration, School of Performing Arts.

Brooklyn College of the City University of New York
Brooklyn, New York 11210
(212) 780-5666

Program: Master of Fine Arts in Performing Arts Management, Department of Theatre.

Columbia University
Center for Theatre Studies
605 Dodge Hall
New York, New York 10027
(212) 280-3408

Program: Master of Fine Arts, theatre-management concentration.

Columbia University
Program in Arts Administration
School of the Arts
615 Dodge Hall
New York, New York, 10027
(212) 280-4331

Program: Master of Fine Arts, arts-administration concentration.

Drexel University
Philadelphia, Pennsylvania 19104
(215) 895-2462

Program: Master of Science in Arts Administration, Center for Multidisciplinary Study and Research.

Golden Gate University
536 Mission Street
San Francisco, California 94105
(415) 442-7000

Program: Certificate of Arts Administration and Master of Arts in Arts Administration, Graduate School of Management.

New York University
777 Education Building
Washington Square
New York, New York 10003
(212) 598-3491

Program: Master of Arts in Arts Administration, School of Education, Health, Nursing, and Arts Professions, Division of Arts and Arts Education.

Rollins College
Roy E. Crummer School of Finance and Business Administration
Winter Park, Florida 32789
(305) 646-2405

Program: Master of Business Administration in Arts Management.

Sangamon State University
Community Arts Management Program
Public Affairs Center
Springfield, Illinois 62708
(217) 786-6535

Program: Master of Arts in Community Arts Management.

State University of New York at Binghamton
Binghamton, New York 13901
(607) 798-2630

Program: Master of Business Administration in the Arts, School of Management.

University of California
Graduate School of Management
Management in the Arts Program
Los Angeles, California 90024
(213) 825-2014

Program: Master of Business Administration in Management of the Arts, Graduate School of Management.

University of Cincinnati
College-Conservatory of Music
Arts Administration Program
Cincinnati, Ohio 45221
(513) 475-4383

Program: Master of Arts in Arts Administration, College Conservatory of Music.

University of Iowa
Hancher Auditorium
Iowa City, Iowa 52242
(319) 353-4717

Program: Master of Fine Arts in Arts Management, Department of Communication and Theatre Arts.

University of Michigan
Department of Theatres and Drama
2550 Frieze Building
Ann Arbor, Michigan 48109
(313) 763-5213

Program: Master of Arts in Theatre Management, Department of Theatre and Drama.

University of Wisconsin-Madison
Center for Arts Administration
1155 Observatory Drive
Madison, Wisconsin 53706
(608) 263-4161

Program: Master of Arts in Arts Administration, Graduate School of Business.

Yale University
School of Drama
222 York Street
New Haven, Connecticut 06520
(203) 436-1589

Program: Master of Fine Arts in Theater Administration.

Publications

ArtSEARCH: The National Employment Service Bulletin for the Performing Arts

ArtSEARCH is a biweekly listing of performing arts employment opportunities, including administration, production, artistic, and educational positions. Annual subscription is $25. To subscribe, write to:

Theatre Communications Group
355 Lexington Avenue
New York, New York 10017

Backstage

Backstage is a weekly newspaper published for the arts and communications industries. It includes news and employment information. It is available on newsstands in various cities or by subscription.

Backstage
330 West 42nd Street
New York, New York 10036

Show Business

Show Business is a weekly newspaper that lists names of agents, names of shows in production, and the names of those to contact for information. It is available on newsstands in major cities or by subscription.

Show Business
Leo Schull Publications
134 West 44th Street
New York, New York 10036

Theatre Communications

Theatre Communications is published monthly by the Theatre Communications Group and contains information and articles on not-for-profit theater activities throughout the nation.

Theatre Communications Group, Inc. (TCG)
355 Lexington Avenue
New York, New York 10017

Theatre Crafts

Theatre Crafts, the magazine for professionals in theater, film, video, and the performing arts is published nine times a year. It contains in-depth reports on all technical aspects of theater and contains articles on management and administration. *Theatre Crafts* often lists educational, internship, union, and career information on its editorial pages and contains much pertinent educational and product advertising.

Theatre Crafts
250 West 57th Street
New York, New York 10017
(Single copies $2.50/annual subscription $17.95)

The Theatrical Calendar

The Theatrical Calendar is a listing of current and future activities in the theater including current shows, openings, previews, tryouts, road companies and off- and off-off Broadway. It provides the names and addresses of producers, general managers, press agents, and advertising agencies, as well as up-to-date schedules. It is available in selected bookstores in New York City (Drama Bookshop, 723 Seventh Avenue or Applause Theatre Books, 100 West 67th Street) or by subscription. *The Theatrical Calendar* is published biweekly.

The Theatrical Calendar
Celebrity Service, Inc.
171 West 57th Street
New York, New York 10019
(Single copies $4.50/one issue monthly for 12 months $50.00/full subscription—every issue for 14 months—$100.00)

The Theatrical Index

The Theatrical Index is a comprehensive listing of New York agents, producers, and theaters, as well as an up-to-date compilation of theatrical productions including schedules, ticket-price scales, recording information, and contacts for producers, general managers, press agents, advertising representatives, and production stage managers. *The Theatrical Index* lists current, up-coming, and possible Broadway and off-Broadway productions and road-tour schedules. It is published weekly.

The Theatrical Index
Price Berkley, publisher
888 Eighth Avenue
New York, New York 10019
(Single copies and subscriptions available through the publisher)

Theatre Profiles

This illustrated guide to America's not-for-profit theater is published by
the Theatre Communications Group and contains complete artistic profiles plus financial and production information for nearly 170 of the United
States's not-for-profit regional theaters. *Theatre Profiles* is illustrated with
production photographs and is an invaluable resource for information on
the nation's not-for-profit theaters.

Theatre Communications Group
355 Lexington Avenue
New York, New York 10017
(Single copy $14.95)

Variety

Variety is published daily by *Daily Variety* in California and weekly by
Weekly Variety in New York. Both provide current information on all
aspects of entertainment, although *Weekly Variety* is probably more relevant to the theater professional, containing reviews, casting information,
information on Broadway and touring box office receipts, and employment information. Both are available on newsstands and through subscription.

Daily Variety
Daily Variety Inc.
1400 N. Cahuenga Blvd.
Hollywood, California 90028

Weekly Variety
Variety Inc.
154 West 46th Street
New York, New York 10036

Index